the
sales
sweet
spot

What People Are Saying About
The Sales Sweet Spot

George Demaree has crafted a practical and insightful guide on the critical role that sales skills play—not just in closing deals, but in building a successful career. *The Sales Sweet Spot* presents a comprehensive approach to mastering the sales process, offering proven strategies, essential knowledge, and core principles that every sales professional and leader should know.

—Al Cornish
Chief Operating Officer
Closing the Gap Consulting LLC

George Demaree is the consummate sales professional, and someone I've admired and counted on over the years for advice about sales, people, and life. And now he has taken the time and effort to record and share the wealth of information he has garnered throughout his professional life. His guidebook will be one you will consult time and time again, no matter where you are along your journey to find that "Sales Sweet Spot."

—Mary R. Harville
President and CEO
Kentucky Lottery Corporation

The Sales Sweet Spot isn't just a book about selling—it's a guide to leading with heart, grit, and purpose. I met George, and what started as a business relationship quickly evolved into a deep friendship grounded in shared values and a commitment to helping young people find meaning and purpose in their lives. His stories are honest, his strategies are practical, and his lessons are rooted in decades of real experience. If you're looking to grow as a sales professional or a leader—or become a more impactful human being—this book will help you find your sweet spot.

—Greg Pestinger
CEO, Pestinger Peak Performance Inc.
Author of the International Best-Selling Book
The Road To Purpose

George Demaree has written a thought-provoking book that serves as an invaluable resource for sales professionals seeking to elevate their sales skills and strategies. From cover to cover, it provides a comprehensive education on becoming an impactful sales leader. Revenue generation is indeed the lifeblood of any business organization, and this book delivers actionable insight for those with a growth-oriented mindset.

—Calvin Ellison
President of The Executive Impact Group

In *The Sales Sweet Spot*, George Demaree has written a book that offers people working in sales-related jobs a roadmap to success—a formula for what it takes to be a standout salesperson and sales leader. His book also gives people the other side of a sales pitch, which is essential: knowledge.

—DeWayne Wickham
Former *USA Today* Columnist
Emmy Award Winner and Founding Dean of the School
of Global Journalism & Communication at
Morgan State University

the
sales
sweet
spot

Proven Principles to Prosper in Sales and Sales Leadership

GEORGE DEMAREE

Publishing support provided by
Ignite Press
55 Shaw Ave. Suite 204
Clovis, CA 93612
www.IgnitePress.us

ISBN: 979-8-9998898-0-5
ISBN: 979-8-9998898-1-2 (Hardcover)
ISBN: 979-8-9998898-2-9 (E-book)

For bulk purchases and for booking, contact:

George Demaree
rrsoulutions1@outlook.com
www.thesalesweetspot.com

Library of Congress Control Number: 2025916218

Cover design by Usman Tariq
Edited by Cathy Cruise
Interior design by Jetlaunch

FIRST EDITION

This book is dedicated to the most extraordinary man I have ever known—my father, George Demaree Sr. He taught me how to be a man, a father, a husband, an uncle, a grandfather, and a friend. He was a high-integrity person who did every-thing by the book and could stretch a dollar. He never made much money, but he built a three-bedroom house in a nice neighborhood, owned two cars, and helped my sister and me through high school and college. He was never late for any-thing. He would say you are late if you are not 15 minutes early. He gave me the shirt off his back and allowed me to use his car to attend summer school while he took the bus to work. I love my children, but that is a significant sacrifice. He gave me the money to pay my utility bill when I didn't have the money to pay. There has never been a time that I can remember when we didn't have all we needed. He was the provider, and my mother was the nurturer. He passed away suddenly on December 3, 2000, and I never had the opportunity to say goodbye and well done. It was the saddest day of my life.

Acknowledgments

I would also like to extend a special thank you to a few of the leaders who supported me throughout my 40-year career in the broadcast sales industry. My first radio sales manager, Jane Vance, decided to add me to her sales team despite my interview attire of a Members Only jacket, a skinny leather tie, and no prior broadcast sales experience. I would like to thank Clear Channel Communications Founder and CEO Lowry Mays and WHAS/WAMZ radio Vice President and General Manager Bob Scherer for making the incredible decision in 1990 to hire me to lead WAMZ's sales team. Thanks to WAMZ Program Director Coyote Calhoun for helping to develop a great sales manager and program director partnership. Dale Schaefer, for hiring me twice when I needed a new opportunity—once as general sales manager for WDJX/WLRS radio and several years later as general sales manager for WGZB/WMJM radio. Brian Elam for the chance to lead the sales team for one of America's premier Adult R&B radio stations, WCFB radio, Orlando, Florida, and my last WAMZ sales manager, Jerry Solomon. My father was a barber, and I would drop by his barbershop every Wednesday afternoon to see him and his friends. It was a safe place where men could laugh, tell jokes, and share stories.

One day Jerry went to my father's barbershop to tell him how much he appreciated the job he had done raising me, saying he had raised a good man. It was one of the kindest things any leader had ever done for me, and it brought my father to tears. Jerry passed away several years ago, and I wish I could have said thank you, Jerry, for displaying the power of leading with kindness. Finally, thanks to Jim Waits Sr., owner of Jim Waits Ford, for believing in me when I needed it the most, and a sales assistant named Melissa who sat at a desk outside my office, overheard many of my one-on-one coaching sessions, and said many times, "You need to write a book."

Table of Contents

Part Two

Part Three

Foreword

There are some books you read and put away. Then there are others, rare ones, that you remember and that you keep within arm's reach because they speak to something deeper than tactics, trends, or temporary tips. *The Sales Sweet Spot* by George Demaree belongs in the latter category. Though framed around the world of sales, this book is really about life—about the kind of character, mindset, and heart that not only leads to closed deals but to opened doors, deep relationships, and lasting success.

George has spent over 29 years leading high-performing sales teams in the radio industry—one of the most competitive and rapidly changing sectors in media. He's trained countless professionals, coached young talent into seasoned leaders, and built a reputation for excellence and integrity. But more than his experience, what makes this book invaluable is George's commitment to principle over personality, purpose over performance, and service over self-promotion.

Reading this book is like walking through the book of Proverbs in the Bible, with a seasoned guide who knows the terrain of human behavior, business negotiations, and relational intelligence. As the saying goes, "Rules are many, principles are few. Rules change, but principles never do." George gives us principles, over 40 of them, that are as timeless as they are timely. Just as the sun rises in the east and water boils at 212°F, these truths remain unshaken. They work across generations, industries, and borders.

At the heart of George's philosophy is a radical shift: Move your mission from selling a product to serving a person. He writes, "You can achieve long-term success if your mission is to help your customer rather than try to sell them something." That's not just good sales advice; that's wisdom for life.

One of George's most powerful insights is his threefold definition of success:

1. The demand for what you do
2. Your ability to do it well
3. The difficulty of replacing you

These three markers—relevance, excellence, and uniqueness—form the foundation of a life that matters and a career that lasts.

I've had the opportunity of knowing George for over 40 years. We were college friends in the mid-'70s, navigating the turbulent waters of youth and early adulthood together. After reading his book, I jokingly told him, "This is the same George I knew in college." And I'm sure he was thinking the same about me. But in truth, this is the same George I knew. The same young man who, after long shifts at McDonald's, would bring back bags of leftover hamburgers to share with broke, hungry college students like me. He did it not for gain, but out of genuine care. That spirit of generosity and people-first thinking has never left him. It simply matured, sharpened, and bore fruit in a career that has blessed an enormous number of people.

This book is more than a compilation of strategies; it's a compass. It will help you find your true North Star in a world of shifting values and bottom-line pressures. So read it. Digest it. Mark it up. Pass it along—and most importantly, live its truths.

Because when you do, you won't just succeed in sales, you'll succeed in life. And you'll discover, just like George has, that your sweet spot has been waiting for you all along.

Kevin Cosby, PhD
Pastor of St. Stephen Baptist Church
President of Simmons College of Kentucky

Letter to My Readers

The number of adults in the United States employed in sales-related jobs varies depending on how those jobs are defined. However, according to the most recent data from the Bureau of Labor Statistics, about 11 percent of people in the US are employed in "sales and sales-related occupations." This includes jobs such as retail sales, wholesale, manufacturing, and real estate sales.

HubSpot states that the average turnover rate in sales-related jobs is 35 percent—substantially higher than in all other industries. This is an example of thousands of people who see the rewards gained from a successful sales career, but did not receive the training or possess the characteristics and discipline to succeed in the long term.

Furthermore, Zappi's research indicates that the success rate of salespeople who consistently meet or exceed sales expectations varies significantly depending on their industry—from as low as 1 percent to slightly over 20 percent. I regard many of them as "sweet spot" seekers.

The Sales Sweet Spot: Proven Principles to Prosper in Sales and Sales Leadership will equip you with the skills necessary to become an exceptional salesperson, sales leader, or manager. The book will consistently remind you of what it takes to find success and the actions required to maintain it.

Nothing is more satisfying for a professional or amateur golfer than hitting the sweet spot with a perfect golf swing. It's the spot on the head of a golf club that's slightly larger than a centimeter. When struck, it will create maximum accuracy and distance. Golfers who love the game spend their entire lives searching for the sweet spot, and if it happens once during any single round of golf, most will say, "That's the swing that keeps me coming back."

Everyone is in search of their sweet spot. But sweet spots are elusive and can be described in several ways depending on your profession. It's the ideal position sought to create phenomenal outcomes—a situation that allows you to be the best you can be. It's recognizing the difference between being the best and being the best that you can be. Every professional endeavor or desire has a sweet spot. Sales and sales leadership are no different.

Sweet spot seeking is a continuous journey. When you think you've arrived, a change can occur, often beyond your control. The change may be physical, technological, resource-based, cultural, or vision-related. All require a "swing adjustment." Finding your sweet spot requires focused discipline and commitment. But the journey can be very gratifying when you have a system and are not afraid to think critically and creatively. This book serves as a roadmap to help you navigate this exciting journey.

In my 40 years as a sales and sales leadership professional, I've concluded that there are two kinds of successful sales professionals: There are those who consistently meet expectations, adhere to the sales process, fulfill all required criteria to achieve their goals and objectives, and do what it takes to keep their job. Then there are those who always focus on exceeding expectations—the **sweet spot seekers**. Like professional golfers, they are constantly seeking an edge, new ideas, and techniques that will propel them past their teammates and competitors.

Introduction:
The Sales Sweet Spot

Your sales and sales leadership sweet spot can be achieved if you take advantage of the principles embedded in the experiences, epiphanies, and stories shared in the book. Sales professionals who are sweet spot seekers understand their value and recognize that their ability to exceed revenue goals consistently will lead to unlimited career opportunities. Every company is in the market for great sales professionals. Earl Nightingale, author of *The Strangest Secret* and a renowned motivational speaker, said, "The demand for what you do, your ability to do it well, and the difficulty of replacing you will determine success."

Consistently delivering outstanding results that exceed expectations will make it difficult for you to be replaced. Many of the ideas and techniques shared in this book can help you gain the edge that moves you from average to good, and possibly great.

There is a cost associated with great success. For-profit and nonprofit industries invest billions of dollars in hiring, training, and nurturing their sales and development teams. According to the *2022 Training Industry Report*, annual expenditures on sales training surpassed $100 billion, decreasing to $98 billion in 2024. Why is the sales success rate as low as 1 percent in some industries, yet billions are invested in sales training annually? And why do some people always seem to achieve their goals and objectives regardless of the market conditions? Those questions will be answered in upcoming chapters.

Are you willing to pay the cost of exceptional success? Professional golfers spend hours perfecting their swing. They hit thousands of balls in various situations to prepare to overcome both hidden and visible obstacles. How much time will you dedicate to refining your sales technique? How hard are you willing to work to acquire a granular understanding of the sales process and its application, to the point where it becomes a part of your muscle memory? Do you have the desire to excel beyond those who consistently produce C+ work and understand that achieving A+ results requires only a small extra effort, done consistently?

The first sales training I received as a newly hired radio salesperson was from a sales trainer who shared, "You need to become a resource for your customers." How do you become a resource for your customers? You will find the answers in this book's upcoming chapters. It will provide the tools to help you understand how to discover and satisfy your customers' needs and concerns. This book enables you to recognize that customers buy for their reasons, not yours.

Don't try to sell a customer a sedan if they want an SUV. I'll share insights on this concept, along with many others I've learned during my sales and sales leadership journey.

This book will also help equip sales leaders with better sales leadership acumen. Sales leadership brings different challenges. You are responsible for coaching, nurturing, problem-solving, and recruiting talent while helping to develop and maintain customer relationships. You also manage your sales team's daily activities and schedule individual one-on-one and team sales meetings. Sales leaders often help create and implement a team's vision, mission, and purpose. You are always under a microscope because your success or failure is documented daily, and the company's success is directly tied to your team's success.

Sales and sales leadership success have a short shelf life. Your long-term success cannot be based on yesterday's accomplishments. It's a reason that sweet spot seeking is a continuous journey. Celebrate your victories, but plan and prepare to conquer next month's goals and objectives. You will quickly discover that you are only a hero for a day. Great sales leaders can satisfy the needs of senior leadership while coaching and nurturing their sales team. It comes with the territory. It's just one of the many circumstances that make sales leadership challenging.

The Sales Sweet Spot will share how several sales professionals, including myself, succeeded in their sales careers. It tackles the challenge of transitioning from a sales team member to a sales team leader, and how your priorities shift from what is best for you to what is best for your team—a move from "me" to "we." It's your ability to remove your ego when making team decisions. The most successful leaders understand the power of humility.

The Sales Sweet Spot is a resource for every salesperson who understands the value of helping customers realize their needs and objectives, and every sales leader who recognizes the power of helping every person on their team to exceed their professional and personal goals. The shared principles, insights, stories, and experiences illustrate the requirements and characteristics necessary for those who aspire to greatness. It helps you recognize that the more you do to help others achieve their goals and objectives, the greater your reward—both financially and in the gratification of positively impacting someone's life.

1

What Triggers an Epiphany?

AN EPIPHANY CAN be triggered by an experience, a conversation, an event, a brainstorming session, or simply a moment alone. Most meaningful accomplishments started with an epiphany—an "aha!" Epiphanies help generate unique ideas and creative solutions. According to a survey conducted by the Reboot Foundation, "Less than 25 percent of people actively seek out opposing viewpoints." They find critical thinking difficult. However, critical thinking can be as simple as following your epiphanies and imagination.

Fear can create an epiphany, and an epiphany can help you overcome fear. Many times, they are interconnected—the aha moment that makes you determined to work through what you fear rather than give up because of what you fear. Fear leads to worry, and most things you worry about never occur, based on my experience. That realization happens through an epiphany, when you realize that faith and fear cannot coexist.

Don't be afraid of failure. Rejection is a part of life for every salesperson, regardless of skill or experience. However, it's essential to recognize that a customer's refusal to purchase your idea, product, or service is typically not a personal rejection of you. The most successful accomplishments often happen after failure. There are several examples of where failure has turned into favor, and where rejection has led to a breakthrough. The experiences, epiphanies, and stories shared in the upcoming chapters will also confirm why you are succeeding or provide tools for future success. If you're struggling to achieve your goals and objectives, the first step is to change the story you tell yourself. It can be the difference between success and failure. Change is difficult, but it starts with a strong belief in your ability to overcome challenges. Many of your future accomplishments are on the other side of fear.

2

The Sales Process

SUSTAINED SUCCESS IS seldom accidental; it requires the discipline to follow a proven sales process. I have observed that there is a common denominator among all successful sales professionals. They all believe they are exceptional salespeople and consider themselves the best in their industry. They believe they consistently hit their sweet spot. Several of my friends are highly successful sales professionals across various sectors, including banking, software, maintenance, insurance, consulting, pharmacy, automobile, and media. If you converse with one or more of them, their passion for the profession quickly comes to the surface. Many struggle to listen because they constantly want to share their opinions. If you listen closely, you will find that they all say many of the same things in different ways.

John fits that category perfectly. He was a highly successful sales professional in the insurance industry. Discussing our sales careers was always a very engaging experience. We shared details about the first sale that gave us the confidence to overcome the challenges associated with a career in sales. I described the steps required to succeed as "The Sales

Process," while John referred to them as "The Sales Cycle." He followed a five-step cycle, while I followed an eight-step process. Regardless of the description, they are both blue-prints for sales success.

Navigating one or more steps of the sales process is a part of your daily sales routine. There will always be wants and needs that require your attention, regardless of the age demographic: the cries of a hungry baby, a teenager trying to convince a parent to use the car, a wife or husband preparing to purchase new furniture or golf clubs, or an employee asking for a salary increase. A sales professional's responsibility is to identify and solve their customers' problems, challenges, needs, and/or wants.

It is also beneficial when a customer emotionally connects with your brand or product. It's when the purchase gives the customer a sense of satisfaction and happiness. Auto dealers understand the importance of offering test drives to qualified buyers—the smell and the ride you experience in a new car can create an emotional connection. The dealer recognizes that the possibility of closing the sale increases the longer the test drive lasts. Engaging customers who are emotionally invested in your cause is essential if you are the director of development for a nonprofit.

John and I both agreed that the process or cycle is both art and science.

Sales is simply a value exchange. Successful sales professionals exhibit the art of creativity, imagination, courage, empathy, integrity, intuition, passion, and critical thinking skills while working within a system that utilizes every step of the sales process.

There is a reason for the significant divide between average, good, and great sales professionals. Great ones understand the art and science of the sales process. They work hard and smart, recognizing the distinction between creating efficiencies and taking shortcuts.

How effective would you be if you had the imagination and creative thinking ability to generate ideas and solutions, but struggled with poor listening skills or were unable to overcome objections?

The sales profession is not for the faint of heart. You may struggle with the uncertainty of a sales career. I worked with a research director who had the best presentation skills of almost everyone on the staff, yet her compensation was a fraction of that of nearly everyone on the sales staff. I strongly suggested she consider moving to the sales team, but she couldn't overcome her fear of failure. The peaks and valleys, accompanied by a sales career and the inconsistency of monthly pay, made her uncomfortable.

Welcome and expect challenges early in your sales career. Maintaining a positive attitude can convert challenges into opportunities for growth and success. Mastering the steps of the sales process will transform surviving into thriving.

The Eight-Step Sales Process:

1. Prospecting and identifying perfect prospects
2. Creating a value proposition that leads to an appointment
3. Facilitating a comprehensive customer needs analysis
4. Developing ideas and solutions
5. Presenting well-prepared ideas and solutions
6. Uncovering and resolving objections
7. Closing the sales
8. Following up after the sales

Review Questions

- What is the first step of your sales process?
- Why is a sales process or sales cycle important?
- What step in the sales process is the most important?
- Do you believe the sales process is an art or a science? Why?
- What is the final step of your sales process, and why is it important?

Part One

3

The Launch

"Every dream begins with a dreamer. Always remember, you have within you the strength, the patience, and the passion to reach for the stars to change the world."

—Harriet Tubman

IT WOULD BE an understatement to say that launching my radio sales career presented significant challenges. There was no formal training program, no sales call observation with a sales manager, and no account list except for an inactive prospect file and the Yellow Pages. I learned many cold-calling techniques while listening to my coworker's phone calls. I tried to use their words and phrases, and did my best not to sound scripted. I called companies that had purchased at least a quarter-page ad in the Yellow Pages, listened to ads on competing radio and TV stations, and cut out ads from our local newspaper. Persistence led to an appointment with a small company in southern Indiana. My only focus was on closing a sale, so I convinced the owner to place an advertising schedule, which I later realized had little to no chance of success. The size of their investment didn't allow for the frequency of impressions needed to succeed. And what made it worse was that they never paid their invoice. It was a valuable learning experience.

No one shared or helped me to understand the Five Sales Success Principles—the first being Your Sales Mission. In summary, the focus should be on addressing the needs of the customer. All five will be explained in more detail in one of the upcoming chapters.

I started to learn the importance of the following six statements:

1. You can't solve a problem that you don't recognize or understand.
2. Helping your customer should be your primary focus.
3. There must be a thorough understanding of the objective and the desired results.
4. The perfect prospect has specific characteristics.
5. Customers buy for their reasons and not yours.
6. There are no shortcuts to success; it requires hard work.

My on-the-job training taught me that I needed a more targeted approach to prospecting. I also learned the importance of reaching the correct decision-makers with a valid value proposition to approach a potential customer and secure an appointment. It is also important to capture your customer's curiosity quickly. Many of my early sales epiphanies were motivated by failure.

The first 12 to 18 months were challenging, but I never lost faith in my ability to succeed. I later realized that it takes approximately 12 to 18 months for most sales professionals to acquire a granular understanding of their products, services, and customer challenges.

My monthly compensation was guaranteed for the first six months, but starting in the seventh month, 100 percent of my compensation was based on the commissions earned. I had taken a pay cut from my previous job, but I believed this was an opportunity to more than triple my income.

There were days when I had at most five dollars, and I had to decide whether to eat lunch or put gas in my car to make sales calls. On one occasion, I had to cross a toll bridge with only a silver dollar my grandfather had given me, and the toll attendant refused to let me pass without paying.

However, my darkest day in the radio sales industry occurred on a cold November night, approximately 12 months after I had begun my career in broadcast sales. I came home and was greeted by disconnected utilities. It was a sobering experience. I could not do many of life's daily routines that we sometimes take for granted. I sat on my couch in the dark, hungry and depressed. I vowed never to allow this to happen again. The cut in salary made it a struggle to pay my bills. It was one of the two most discouraging days of my career in broadcast sales. I considered quitting, but I had invested 12 months on the streets, had started to develop meaningful relationships, and had a four-year-old son.

Looking back on those days, I realized it is the price you pay to succeed. Difficult situations always accompany every great accomplishment. The question is, Will you see it through, or will you allow the problem to get the best of you?

Failure was not an option. It was a test of my resolve and faith in God.

Your ability to persevere during challenging times is the key to achieving long-term success. It begins with believing that your current situation will not be your permanent situation.

Review Questions

- What's a common mistake traditional salespeople make?
- Have you ever targeted a customer for the wrong reasons? If so, why?
- How long did it take for you to become comfortable with your product or service?
- How did you overcome a challenge that seemed insurmountable?
- Which sales activities delivered the best results?

4

The Quest

---

*"The tragedy of life doesn't lie in not reaching your goal.
The tragedy lies in having no goal to reach."*

—Benjamin Mays

*The determined effort during the pursuit should
reflect the value of your pursuit.*

CALVIN WAS A member of a radio sales team, and he possessed many of the necessary characteristics to succeed. He was a tenacious prospector and would work tirelessly to secure appointments. His effort helped him schedule an appointment with one of his team's most elusive customers. Calvin realized that if he could convince the customer to reduce their budget commitment to social media ads and replace it with his radio stations, it could lead to achieving his revenue objective for the entire year.

Calvin was well-prepared. He facilitated a thorough needs analysis and made several in-person site visits while working to generate fresh ideas. He was so excited about the opportunity and so confident that he would close the sale that he began imagining how the customer would benefit and what he could purchase with the future commissions he would earn.

However, the customer thanked him for his effort but rejected his proposed solutions. He returned to the office both dejected and discouraged. Calvin was asked if he understood the reason for the customer's decision. He said he wasn't sure. He believed it was the cost of his proposed solution, but felt there was another reason. The customer liked Calvin and his ideas, but social media had produced good results.

Calvin lost the sale because he failed to ask the correct questions—questions that not only identified needs but also helped to sift out objections.

One of the first gifts I received from management during my early years as a radio salesperson was a coffee mug inscribed with the quote: "Salesmanship begins when a customer says no." Calvin's sales manager told him there is never an opportunity to overcome an objection if the objection is not understood.

Successful sales professionals have many of the same characteristics as successful investigative news reporters. Successful news reporters are tenacious, curious, and stick-to-it-ive. They know how to probe, have the courage to ask difficult questions, and understand that their effectiveness depends on their ability to find information their audience considers valuable and entertaining.

Successful sales professionals exhibit the same characteristics. They probe and ask good questions, understanding that their effectiveness depends on their ability to analyze their customers' needs, desires, problems, and challenges.

Your ability to ask strategically relevant, well-positioned, open-ended questions will make the difference between success and failure. It will also give you all the necessary information to help your customers.

Good questions lead to good answers, which in turn lead to more good questions. If you were to ask your customer, "What issues keep you up at night?" the customer might respond, "Exploring a strategy to reduce my first-quarter customer attrition rate." This answer could lead to several questions starting with the words *who*, *what*, *why*, *where*, or *how*. Questions like: What are the characteristics of your primary customers? How would your customers rate their buying experience? How were customers introduced to your business? What would your customers say are the deciding benefits they seek and gain when purchasing your product? Why is the first quarter the most challenging? How is your budget planned—calendar or fiscal year?

However, be strategic when using questions that begin with the word *why*. Questions starting with the word *why* can be perceived as a parent-to-child conversation. *Why* is the word your parents used when addressing what they believed was questionable behavior. Instead, replace *why* questions with *how* questions. *How* questions are viewed as more empathetic, unintrusive, and comfortable compared to *why* questions, which can be perceived as interrogative and aggressive.

There will be times when a customer will decide not to use your product or service despite your hard work and your belief that the offer you presented is a better solution than your competitors'. These are the times when you need the ability to uncover hidden objections. Uncovering hidden objections requires the courage and skill to ask the correct questions at the correct time strategically. Never leave an appointment, no matter your perception of its effectiveness, without asking your customer the following question: "Can you think of a reason why you won't take my call on our agreed-upon date and time?" If there is a hidden objection, it will usually surface after asking this question. If your customer asks, "Why do you ask?" be transparent and tell them, "I never want to leave an appointment, especially one that went as well as ours, without completely understanding my customers' needs."

There are two types of "no's": no's that mean "not yet" and can be used to help you later, and no's that completely shut the door because you don't understand why.

Understanding how you succeed and how you fail are both critical. Success can be as simple as repeating activities that bring success and avoiding those that lead to failure. Neither happens by accident.

Review Questions

- How did you react when you lost a sale you were sure you would close?
- What is one of your favorite questions during a customer's needs meeting?
- What technique have you used to uncover hidden objections?
- What is the first question you ask when a customer says no?
- When have you used rejection as a springboard for success?

5

The Five Sales Success Principles

Procedures without principles are like a building with no foundation.

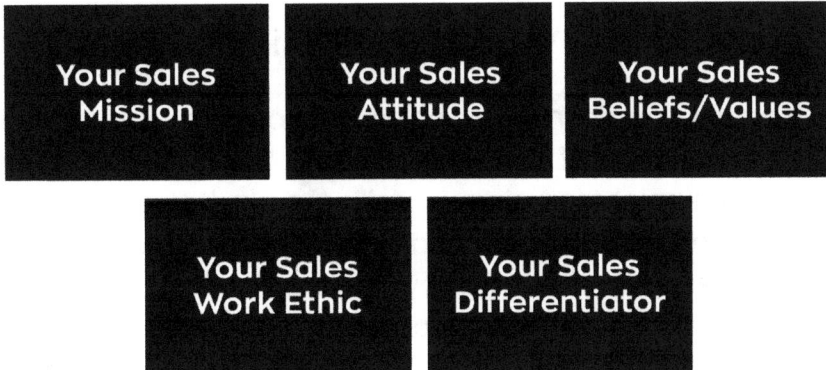

Your Sales Mission	**Your Sales Attitude**	**Your Sales Beliefs/Values**

Your Sales Work Ethic	**Your Sales Differentiator**

CALVIN WAS CONFIDENT, courageous, and of high character, but he lacked the competence to deliver a successful result. The previous chapter shared the reasons he failed to close an important sale. Each step of the sales process is like a piece of a jigsaw puzzle; each piece is equally important.

Because of his positive attitude, Calvin succeeded despite the temporary setback. His positive mindset enabled him to use setbacks as a setup for a comeback. Both failure and success are temporary, based on how you view them. Success and failure are interconnected. Both are primarily the result of habit. The Five Sales Success Principles comprise the DNA of all successful sales professionals. Calvin not only understood each principle, but he put each one into practice.

Your sales mission, attitude, beliefs/values, work ethic, and differentiator are the foundations of successful sales professionals. They help to determine your why and purpose. If asked, you will discover that successful sales professionals adhere to every principle and never focus solely on themselves.

The Five Sales Success Principles will help shape your thinking during good and challenging times.

1. Your Sales Mission

How would you define your sales mission? You can achieve long-term success if your mission is to help your customers rather than solely focusing on selling a product or service. I have worked with and been sold by salespeople whose primary mission was profit-making. They didn't realize that getting what you want depends on helping others get what they want. Most people can sense when you are concerned about their issues. I've also worked with sales professionals whose mission was to satisfy customers' needs. They provide customer service that exceeds expectations, typically receive a larger share of the budget than their competitors, and have opportunities for repeat business and referrals. Relationships are developed when your mission is to help satisfy your customers' needs.

2. Your Sales Attitude

Calvin loved his job. He came to work every day with a smile and a sense of optimism. He didn't allow negative results or negative people to determine his happiness, and recognized that two of the only things he could control were his mood and his attitude. Be a glass-half-full person. Face adversity with a smile and grace. Be that person who never seems to have a bad day. Positive people have a knack for extracting the best from all situations. They are the first to volunteer to help people in need and consider it a privilege to help someone succeed.

A positive attitude helps fuel creativity and imagination, making it easier to conduct business. Reach out to a satisfied customer to share a new idea or check on their progress. There is nothing more rewarding than the feeling you get when you help someone else.

Sometimes you must do something you've never done to get something you never had.

3. Your Sales Beliefs and Values

Calvin believed in his product. He felt his proposed solution could meet his customers' needs and deliver superior results. Although his cost was higher than his competitor's, he had a well-defined competitive advantage. But could the advantage deliver value exceeding expectations? Was there the possibility of measurable results that would justify the cost? And could that story be effectively communicated to his customer? He not only believed in his product and solutions, but he also believed in himself. Calvin had a high level of self-esteem, but was not seen as arrogant. Few things are more valuable than integrity and your ability to earn trust. What are you willing to sacrifice to help your customers? Sometimes you must do something you've never done to get something you never had.

4. Your Sales Work Ethic

You reap what you sow. Rewards are earned by those willing to invest the time, work hard, and be disciplined enough to adhere to the process. Nick Saban, legendary college football coach, said, "Suffer the pain of discipline or you will suffer the pain of disappointment." Calvin didn't shy away from hard work. He was a tenacious hunter. He employed several innovative techniques to reach potential decision-makers. He sent a customer a Louisville Slugger baseball bat with the customer's name inscribed on the bat and a note that read, "Our partnership will hit your results out of the park." He worked nontraditional hours and never ended the day without sending a thank-you note to one of his current or potential customers. The latest research indicates that fewer than 30 percent of emails are opened, compared to a 90 percent open rate for US postal mail. He was working when everyone else was playing. He liked to play as much as anyone else, but he understood that hard work and the time to play are interdependent. Are you the first person in your office and the last to leave? The margin of success is very slim. He took full advantage of "the power of one more," which we'll discuss in Chapter 8.

5. Your Sales Differentiator

Differentiating yourself is easier than it seems. Calvin didn't use his teammates as examples. There were current things he felt he could emulate, but he realized that to be the best, you need to do things others refuse to do. He used his mission, attitude, beliefs, values, and work ethic to differentiate himself from his competitors and teammates. He didn't put guardrails on his potential. He had a unique style, and his customers loved him. People who experience great success are always looking for opportunities to improve. When you are the best, your competition will try their best to take you down. Dare to be different. The only way to coast is downhill; the scenery never changes if you are not leading the pack. Being the best requires being different from the rest.

Calvin didn't let one failure define him or his ability to be a successful sales professional. He used his failure as a learning opportunity and continued to employ the same sales process that had helped him gain an audience with a critical decision-maker. By the way, he returned to the customer who had rejected his proposed initial solutions and continued giving him the same attention he gave to his best customers. Six months later, Calvin adjusted the proposal, overcame the objection, and the customer became one of his best revenue producers.

> **Being the best requires being different from the rest.**

Review Questions

- Which sales principle has helped shape your thinking the most?
- How do your actions reflect your values?
- How strongly do you believe in your product or service?
- What are examples of your daily activities that produce the best results?
- What do you believe differentiates you from your teammates and competitors?

6

Success C-Word
Characteristics

"A leopard can't change its spots, though they might fade a little."

—Unknown

As a sales professional, getting your first sale worthy of attention is like your rite of passage. It's the confirmation you needed that helped you persevere while improving your sales and industry competence.

For me, it was a radio marketing campaign bought by Jim Waits Sr., the owner of Jim Waits Ford in Oldham County, Kentucky. Jim wanted to use radio to promote his unique positioning statement: "Cars, like eggs, are cheaper in the country." WAMZ radio was his favorite station, as well as the favorite of most of his customers and employees. Jim called the station and spoke to our sales manager, and she decided to send me to answer his questions. It was a 35-minute ride from downtown Louisville. When I arrived at the dealership, Jim was busy working on his floor plan and had me wait for over an hour before he invited me into his office. I used that time to meet everyone on his staff: the receptionist, who happened to be his wife, the sales team, and their service staff. I was confident that I could succeed as a radio salesperson and that I possessed the courage to overcome many of the stereotypes associated with country music and the people who loved the format.

Jim talked to me for over two hours from the moment I walked into his office. He shared stories about the dealership, challenging market conditions, and his family, most of whom worked for the dealership. Jim had created a low-pressure sales environment, and the people of Oldham and the surrounding counties loved him. He said, "Either I like you, or I don't like you, and if I don't like you, you couldn't sell me $50 bills for a quarter." He believed I was a person of high character and could be trusted. The experience provided a valuable epiphany: Successful people often enjoy talking about themselves; developing active listening skills can help you build strong relationships.

I presented two sales opportunities totaling $7,000 created by my sales manager. Jim thought about it and decided to buy both. I could hardly contain myself. Why did Jim make that decision? It wasn't because of some unique ability to close. He was sold on the radio station long before I walked onto his showroom floor. But why did he buy me?

It's the rewards you receive when you exhibit a positive attitude, a likable personality, and an eagerness to listen and understand your customers' goals, objectives, and challenges. Recognition is a great motivator. Active listening skills demonstrate empathy and can be used as a differentiator. He noticed my patience and the courage I showed in meeting his team members while waiting to speak to him.

The confidence, courage, and character exhibited during those three hours at Jim's dealership helped me overcome my lack of radio sales experience and competence.

Proper coaching and experience will improve your competence. Your attitude influences your confidence and courage. Character has more to do with your morals, ethics, beliefs, and values.

Competence Your sales skill	**Confidence** Your self-esteem
Courage Your mental toughness	**Character** Your honesty/integrity

Competence: Every sales career should begin with a comprehensive sales training program that equips you with a thorough understanding of the sales process.

When interviewing for a sales industry opportunity, ask if the company provides sales training during your initial employment period. Preferably, a minimum of 30 days. Training is essential, regardless of your level of expertise or years of experience. Different companies and sales directors have different expectations. If they lack or have an incomplete sales training process, look for information in books and periodicals, ask insightful questions during one-on-ones with your sales managers, or seek help from other sales team members by listening and asking for guidance. The most effective way to confidently launch your sales career is to be trained by a sales training expert. There are occasions when success requires an investment of time and money.

You only have one chance to make a first impression. Your customers will quickly recognize your competence level, usually during your approach. Research, read, study, practice, and learn from your mistakes. One of your goals should be to improve at least one step of the sales process daily.

Confidence: Confidence is your belief in yourself and the opportunity you represent. When you know beyond a shadow of a doubt, you can help someone and understand what's required. Your competence will help build your confidence. It's also your ability to follow your intuition. Customers sense confidence in the same way they sense your competence. Customers will only buy your product or service when they are confident you can help solve their problems and challenges. Confidence is not cocky, arrogant, bolstered, or conceited.

> **The best way to conquer fear is to do what you fear.**

Don't give the impression of being a know-it-all. Humility is one of the most powerful attitudes you can possess.

Courage: Courage differs from confidence, yet one supports the other. Courage is your ability to overcome fear. It's your risk tolerance, willingness to ask tough questions, and ability to uncover objections both on the surface and below. It takes courage to be different and stand for your beliefs and values. The best way to conquer fear is to do what you fear. Don't let the fear of failure stifle your dreams. Being courageous is inspirational. It stimulates almost every sense in your body. It helps you to realize your purpose.

Character: Your character is defined by your convictions and principles. It's doing the right thing when nobody is watching, and your eagerness to keep your word. It's your honesty, trust-worthiness, and integrity. When you earn trust, you guard it like a precious jewel. Character means taking responsibility, regardless of the results or consequences. Winning is import-ant, but not at the cost of compromising who you are. You can't hide your character.

Review Questions

- What strategies have you used to increase your sales competence?
- Can you point to a sale or event that grew your sales confidence?
- Do you consider yourself courageous? Share a few examples.
- What are the characteristics of a high-character person?
- Can you share a time when courage was required to achieve a goal?

7

Positive Momentum

Momentum can be the reason for success or failure.

POSITIVE MOMENTUM CAN be both inspiring and motivating. It is when your actions produce extraordinary results. It is analogous to a football team consistently making first downs, culminating in touchdowns, or a golfer consistently reaching the green in regulation, resulting in pars and birdies.

The success of our marketing campaigns inspired several new customers to consider adding our radio station to their marketing strategy, and many became consistent marketing partners, while others utilized the station for special promotions. While people often support underdogs, they tend to follow only top dogs. And we became the market leader.

Positive momentum has a way of duplicating itself. It's a driving force. Momentum builds over time when your mindset, habits, and actionable activities create and maintain sustained success. My business plan was working, and the majority of my objectives were being achieved. My passion to help my customers and my adherence to the sales process delivered results. I developed a good reputation and understood its value.

A great workplace culture can promote the positive momentum needed to consistently position your team members to reach and exceed their personal and team sales objectives. However, momentum is fragile. When achieving your goals, avoid slowing down or taking a break. Sales results often slow down without warning. Don't take Friday off if you reach your sales objectives early in the month. I'm not saying you shouldn't take advantage of holidays and vacations. Everyone needs time to recharge. But maintaining positive momentum can be more challenging than the activity required to get it started. Various controlled and uncontrolled factors can impede or halt your progress.

I began my sales leadership career at a well-established radio station with a very skilled team, which led to early success in my sales management career. I did not recognize that I started to believe success was more about me and not as much about my team or customers. Sometimes, success can cause you to lose focus on the fundamentals and the process that got you there. I allowed my staff to make concessions and excuses without adhering to our culture of accountability. A senior station leader once told me that people respect what you inspect, which includes regular self-evaluation. Unproductive habits can gradually become ingrained in an organization's culture, and the team is likely to reflect the characteristics and personality of its leader. Our results started to suffer, and we had to work extra hard to get back on track.

Momentum can also suffer because of uncontrolled variables. It can be as drastic as an economic recession, resulting in job losses and bankruptcies, or as precise as a competitive shift brought about by new technology.

For years, our radio station had format exclusivity and the largest total audience in our Metro Survey Area until a competitor emerged. This forced a strategy adjustment to maintain our momentum.

So take full advantage of those variables you can control. Variables that include your discipline, courage, effort, and grit. Momentum affects all eight steps of the sales process. Starting with your enthusiastic approach to prospecting and your empathic approach to your sales follow-up. Strive to be one of the few people who can thrive during slow periods. Today's results reflect yesterday's activities.

Review Questions

- Can you share a time when you experienced sustained positive momentum?
- What contributed to the experience?
- What strategies did you use to maintain your momentum?
- What factors impeded or hindered your progress?
- How often do you self-evaluate?

8

The Power of One More

"One more" can be the difference between surviving and thriving.

AFTER ABOUT 18 months of faithfully following the sales process, my hard work started to pay dividends. My strategic plan was working, and I began to explore every opportunity to amplify my efforts and expand the number of accounts in my sales pipeline. I realized that a more effective time management strategy would be a valuable differentiator while creating more opportunities.

Approach your sales career with enthusiasm, as if you were a business owner. If you were responsible for managing expenses and revenue to maintain and grow your business, would you work eight-hour days, five days a week? Successful sales professionals never stop prospecting or exploring opportunities to help their customers. They take advantage of the adage, "Success can be realized when preparation meets opportunity."

I discovered the possibility of reaching primary decision-makers was much higher before 8:00 a.m. and after 5:00 p.m. Most of my competitors and teammates started their day after 8:30 a.m. and finished by 5:00 p.m. It was a valuable epiphany.

There was a salesperson on staff at my sister radio station who was one of the best broadcast sales professionals I had the pleasure of knowing. He left used newspapers and periodical clippings scattered like breadcrumbs everywhere, from his cubicle to the break room and the men's room. He never wasted a moment.

This was when I began to understand "the power of one more" and how it could pay dividends. Most successful people possess a competitive attitude and explore every possible opportunity to get an edge on the competition. Achieving management's goals and objectives should never be your only inspiration. Sweet spot seekers work hard and smart to be the best they can be, and they are inspired to be the best. Make being the best a part of your long-term vision.

Our sales manager created a weekly list of individual and team sales results, which was posted on the wall in our sales arena for everyone to see. There were seven people on the sales staff, and I was at the bottom for months. It always left me with a sense of emptiness when one of my teammates used the list to highlight accomplishments. I used their feedback as motivation, and was determined to move up the list. A key part of my growth strategy involved making at least one extra sales call or developing one new idea for a current or potential customer every day. It was an achievable strategy and gave me a win every day. It also created a positive mindset to help me persevere during difficult times. The power of one more is an actionable tactic that is not difficult to initiate if you have the discipline and an understanding of linear growth.

How often does anyone do at least one more than they said they would do? Doing one more not only helps you reach your goals and objectives, it also helps you build positive customer relationships.

Tiny increments often determine success. The margin of success can be very slim.

The difference between first and eighth place in the 100-meter race during the 2024 Olympics was less than 1.2 tenths of a second: 9.79 vs. 9.91. First- and second-place times were nearly identical.

The book *212: The Extra Degree*, written by Mac Anderson and Sam Parker, demonstrates that water maintains its natural state at 211°F, but when adding an extra degree, it turns into steam, which can power a locomotive. A small amount of resistance often causes most people to stop trying, unaware that their breakthrough is just one step away.

....

Every person has an equal amount of time. Success and failure are primarily dependent on how that time is used.

....

About eight months later, after I had followed the sales process for 26 months, one of my teammates noticed that I had moved up to third place on the list. She congratulated me on my progress, but I told her my goal was to be number one. Less than two years later, I reached my goal and became the top direct business salesperson on staff. Every person has an equal amount of time. Success and failure are primarily dependent on how that time is used.

Review Questions

- What is your time management strategy?
- What sales activities help to create the best results?
- How do you use your competitive spirit as a motivator?
- How can you utilize the power of one more to help achieve your sales goals and objectives?
- When have small wins produced big victories?

9

Successful Price Negotiations

*People will pay the price to solve their problems
or satisfy their perceived needs.*

SOME PRICE NEGOTIATIONS are not negotiations at all. They are take it or leave it. During the latter stage of my sales leadership career, one of the market's top media-buying customers would invite representatives from TV and radio to negotiate rates for their upcoming fiscal year. It was not actually a negotiation; they informed each of us about the amount they would pay per commercial, and specified where and in which programs they wanted their commercials to be placed. They didn't want to hear a pitch on value or reasons why we felt our inventory was worth more than they were willing to pay. It was a nonnegotiable meeting. In addition, if you walked away, they would not allow you to reconsider your decision until the following year.

I walked away in the first year, but most of my competitors accepted their terms. Our competitive advantage couldn't overcome their rate objection; they only allowed access once a year, so it was impossible to build a relationship. This was intentional, and quantifying the results for the customer was challenging due to the extensive volume of their media purchases. It was not a complete win-lose relationship because they were investing a significant amount of money. It forced me to find a way to make their rates work or to achieve our revenue objectives without their money.

This example is not the norm. Most negotiations are more interactive. The goal is to create win-win solutions. Cost can be secondary if your solution offers a significant competitive advantage and meets or exceeds the objective.

People want to feel they receive great value for their money. It is more about how you make your customers feel than most people realize. Very few motivators are more important than creating an emotional connection with your customers, making them feel emotionally connected to your product. Analyzing customer needs should also help determine their price tolerance.

To negotiate successfully, you must have answers to the following questions:

- Do you have a competitive advantage?

  This can be an advantage based on a specific feature, like better ratings, or based on an intangible, like superior service.

- How great is their need?

  When the need is overwhelming, the customer has little or no choice but to buy your product. It's like the need to buy a format-exclusive radio station or a network-exclusive TV program, or like the need to have your HVAC system repaired on Saturday at midnight.

- Can you quantify the results?

  This is when the results from the purchase can be directly attributed to your product.

- Is there, or can you create, an emotional attachment?

  These are those occasions when your customer has a personal attachment to your product. Sometimes a new car can create an emotional attachment.

- Does your product's or service's value or preserved value exceed expectations?

  This is when the customers feel the price offered is below their expectations. It's also essential that you do not undervalue your product.

- How effectively can the value proposition be communicated?

  Can the unique benefits and their problem-solving capabilities be effectively communicated? For example, "My product will increase your profit margin by a minimum of 10 percent."

- What is your customer's definition of a win?

  This is when you know without a doubt what winning looks like to your customer. For example, "I will not be happy unless your product increases my profit margin by at least 10 percent."

Negotiation Tips

- Never make the first concession.
- When you make a concession, always get something in return.
- Develop a quick understanding of how your customer negotiates.
- Use silence during negotiations as much as possible.
- Know your numbers. What does a win-win look like from your perspective?
- Be like a point guard. Be quick; don't rush.
- Consider long-term as well as short-term.
- Be willing to walk away.

Price is always one of the primary objections a sales professional will experience. Be prepared to negotiate the price; it's a regular part of the sales process.

Review Questions

- What is your negotiation style?
- Do you consider negotiating challenging? If so, how?
- Can you describe a time when your ability to negotiate created a win-win outcome?
- Can you share a time you made a too-quick concession when negotiating?
- Have you ever turned down a lucrative opportunity because of the terms?

10

Service After the Sale

The opportunity to secure repeat business often depends on your ability to provide service beyond expectations.

MY WIFE AND I had dinner at a moderately priced restaurant and were very impressed with the level of service we received before, during, and after our meal. Peter, our waiter, was pleasant, well-informed, and very detailed. His description of their menu selections made every item appealing. He thanked us for choosing his restaurant while also taking the time to discover our tastes and offering helpful suggestions. Peter went so far as to allow us to sample the soup before we placed our order. The service was prompt, and you could see steam billowing off the food when it arrived at our table. He asked if we were happy during dinner, and before he offered to bring our check. Peter made dining a memorable experience. The restaurant has become one of our favorites, and we always make sure that Peter is our waiter. He has the unique ability to make you feel as though you are his most important customer, even as he serves three other tables simultaneously.

Your service after the sale should give your customers the same feeling Peter gave my wife and me, mainly because it exceeded our expectations. As a sales professional like Peter, you have the power to make every transaction a memorable experience. And that is what it's all about: helping your customers solve their problems and realize their wants, needs, and desires.

Why would you excel at the first seven steps of the sales process but not work as hard to continue the relationship? It's tough to grow your business if you're heavily reliant on generating new business. The media sales industry is highly fluid, so reducing your yearly attrition rate to 25 percent or less would provide an excellent opportunity to achieve your future revenue objectives.

Always make yourself available to your customers and try to help when they are purchasing other products. Focus on your customers' success, ask for their weekly sales results, and offer to help make necessary changes. I occasionally provide incentives for my customers' staff and make a point to get to know them—from the receptionist to the managers, checkout clerks, maintenance staff, and sales team. Being kind and thoughtful is very powerful, and the benefits are immeasurable. Acknowledge the importance of gatekeepers. I recognize birthdays, hobbies, and holidays, and constantly seek opportunities to differentiate myself from the competition.

Peter created a memorable experience. Work to provide the same level of satisfaction to every customer who purchases your service or product.

Review Questions

- How does it make you feel when what you purchase exceeds expectations?
- When was the last time a service you received exceeded expectations?
- What are you willing to do to keep your current customers?
- How much effort is required to replace a valuable customer?
- How do you help celebrate your customers' big moments?

11

Multiply and Diversify

You can either be a change facilitator or a change recipient, but be assured, things will change.

RICK WAS ONE of his team's top revenue producers. His team members could always depend on him to help them achieve their overall revenue objectives. He had outstanding relationships with his customers, many of whom used several of his company's products and services. However, Rick potentially had a problem. He had only 15 active accounts on his list, each representing a significant portion of the team's total revenue. Management emphasized the importance of multiplying and diversifying account lists, highlighting the benefits of adding new potential accounts to the sales pipeline. Losing one account for any reason would be difficult for Rick to overcome. But losing two or more would be disastrous. It would be months before he could replace the revenue, if it could be replaced at all. Additionally, it would require his teammates to compensate for the deficit.

However, the management team hesitated to challenge Rick due to his strong customer relationships and fear of losing him from the team. The country's economic situation declined, resulting in three of Rick's customers terminating their contracts, while the remaining 12 reduced their budgets, some by as much as 50 percent. They could not depend on other salespeople to compensate for the deficit because many faced the same problem.

Megan had the opposite strategy. She also had an outstanding relationship with her customers, but she had over 40 active accounts on her list, none representing more than 8 percent of her total revenue. She had identical economic challenges, but losing a few accounts was not nearly as dramatic.

Multiplying and diversifying your account list is like diversifying your investment portfolio. Never put all your eggs in one basket—or 15, as was the case with Rick.

The auto industry was my primary account target, but I quickly understood the importance of adding customers from different product categories. I had to identify business categories with the same target demographic as most auto dealers and our radio stations. Two of those businesses were a discount retailer and a hardware store. They became two of my top revenue producers.

Diversifying your accounts requires you to service and build relationships with diverse customer personalities as well as products. We will dive deeper into the importance of personality recognition in later chapters.

Many of my customer relationships grew well beyond a business relationship. I knew their families, and we met socially for dinners, concerts, outings on their boats, and many rounds on the golf course. It's one of the reasons I was able to maintain and grow my business, even as other staff members struggled.

During one of those occasions, I received a call from our founder and CEO. He asked, "How did you manage to grow your business while many of your teammates faced chal-lenges?" I considered this, and explained that it was due to my diverse direct customer list and established customer relationships.

I had become what my first sales trainer said I had to become to succeed: a trusted resource for my customers. They valued my opinions, and I helped them understand the importance of maintaining a consistent marketing strategy in good and chal-lenging times. Completely stopping their marketing strategy would do more harm than good. We adjusted their plan during those tough times and focused on increasing their share of available business. It proved to be a good strategy, putting my customers in a great position compared to their competitors when economic conditions improved.

Review Questions

- What strategy do you use to multiply and diversify your account list?
- What are some examples of times your customers con-sidered you a resource?
- When has your ability to adjust/change delivered re-sults? Give an example.
- Have you ever closed a sale from a customer no one else considered?
- Can you describe an occasion when your recommen-dations helped a struggling customer?

12

Self-Awareness

Realizing that YOU are all YOU need is a fear eliminator.

I HAD BEEN in the radio sales business for almost two years when my general manager taught me a valuable lesson about authenticity: Simply be yourself. I was starting to close several new accounts, so I thought buying a pair of cowboy boots would help me fit in with my customers. He said, "You simply need to be yourself. People can see right through fake people. Trust me, it will work." I later realized he wanted me to be authentic. I didn't need to wear cowboy boots or hats to succeed.

Self-evaluation has always been a component of my personal growth strategy. It helps to have an unbiased understanding of your strengths, weaknesses, opportunities, and threats.

Enthusiasm Creates Excellence

When you love what you do professionally, you will experience a sense of freedom that will unleash genuine enthusiasm. It isn't easy to explain. It's an emotional connection to your job. You are both inspired and motivated. Trust me when I say that your customers and teammates can feel as well as see your enthusiasm. I challenge people to find a career that will fuel their enthusiasm. The most successful sales professionals keep it real while enthusiastically exploring every option to help their customers. And when your passion includes helping others, you will never work another day in your life.

There are times when asking for help is your only option. The need for help and the motivation to help are integral to growth and success. Help is a very powerful word. If you ask for help, almost everyone will listen. It can move mountains if used strategically and with integrity. Avoid asking for help if it is not necessary. Don't cry wolf if the wolf doesn't exist.

A sales career can become fun, and almost all our customers have been rewarded with outstanding results. I made sure that the first three questions I asked myself every morning after giving thanks to God were:

1. Who can I help?
2. How can I help?
3. Where can I help?

Your enthusiasm can be the source of epiphanies and creative ideas. On one occasion, while employed as a TV station salesperson, I sent half a pizza to the advertising director of a jewelry store. I made certain it would arrive at 11:30 a.m., right before lunchtime. I asked the deliverer to add a note on the empty side of the pizza box that said, "Don't settle for half the pie. Consider my station."

It worked because it was a unique approach. That afternoon, I received a call informing me that the owner wanted to schedule a meeting. The following month, we were added to their marketing campaign. It marked the beginning of a strong relationship with one of our most challenging advertisers and media representatives.

Success inspires zeal for improvement. I took advantage of every opportunity to improve, whether it was through training, networking, seeking mentors, or reading sales-related books and periodicals. I asked for critical feedback from many of my customers. They were impressed that I asked, and were more than willing to help. I had a customer volunteer to help me with my sales presentation. It was another valuable differentiator.

Review Questions

- What inspires you to succeed?
- How do you use your strengths as an advantage?
- How do you manage your weaknesses?
- What strategy do you use to take advantage of your opportunities?
- What strategy do you use to minimize threats?

13

The Perfect Customer

Time and choices are not mutually exclusive. Your wise or foolish choices will determine how you spend your time.

STAN WAS THE general manager of a popular retail chain that never used radio as a part of their marketing strategy. They bought a number of digital media platforms and commercial space on news and primetime TV. Marie, a senior radio sales account manager, made it a mission to share the value of adding radio and how its ability to tell a story could help enhance their current marketing strategy. She used every option to get an appointment, including phone calls, text messages, letters full of industry information, and drop-bys at their retail locations. Marie talked to their employees, including the local management staff and some customers. She discovered the reasons why customers chose them over their competitors. That was the information that persuaded Stan to give her an appointment.

Their meetings were successful, and Marie believed she had addressed his objections. She knew his company had the budget to add radio to their marketing mix based on their current media spend. However, an unforeseen issue arose. She did not realize that Stan did not control the advertising budget. He was more of a gatekeeper of the budget rather than its facilitator. Stan had never shared that information until she asked for the order. This was before she thoroughly understood how to uncover hidden objections. She never asked, "Are there other people involved in marketing decisions, and if so, how?"

My first radio sales customer was unsuccessful because he had a limited marketing budget, which didn't allow the number of impressions necessary to succeed. I had met with his company several times and never asked the correct questions about their budget. I believe they agreed to meet with me because they enjoyed the attention. It was a complete waste of my time, and they never paid their invoice. Both were learning experiences and a source of valuable epiphanies.

You are wasting your time if your target customers don't possess the five characteristics of the perfect target customer. The perfect customer has all the characteristics needed to become part of your sales pipeline. Identifying the perfect customer is one of the most crucial aspects of the sales process.

The requirements needed to be identified as a perfect target customer start with their ability to pay the cost for your solutions, followed by your ability to reach and speak to the buying decision-maker. Next, do you have a product or service that can satisfy your customers' needs, wants, and/or challenges? Though not as essential as the first three requirements, it's a massive benefit if you have a competitive advantage and the opportunity to solicit referrals.

While on the streets, I found that almost all of my customers met every characteristic of a perfect target customer:

1. They had large marketing budgets compared to most other categories.

2. Decision-makers were available.
3. The audience matched my customer's target demographic.
4. There was a strong competitive advantage.
5. Getting a referral or testimonial was not challenging.

Budget Available

Can they pay the cost without pain or strain? Avoid the small/no-budget customers. They will waste your time if you allow it. Rule of thumb: Spend 80 percent of your time with the 20 percent of your customers who deliver, or have the potential to deliver, 80 percent of your revenue. It usually takes as much time to request large budgets as it does to request small budgets. There are generally only two reasons a business doesn't spend money to solve a problem or improve their product: It's either because of their limited budget, or because they don't believe they need to spend the money. The first is more obvious, but the second is usually due to a lack of competition or the perception that their business can grow organically. Work hard and work smart. Trust your intuition; you will often find that it's correct.

Develop the ability to recognize individuals who pretend to be in charge.

The Buying Decision-Maker

It's a waste of time if you cannot get an audience with someone who can write the check. Do your homework. Use all social media platforms. Develop the ability to recognize individuals who pretend to be in charge. They might have a title, but titles are meaningless if the person doesn't have the power to make the buying decision. It could be a relative or close friend of the customer. Often, they are the actual gatekeepers. It takes courage and confidence to ask the correct questions.

The Ability to Solve the Problem

Can your product or service solve your customers' issues or challenges? Does it provide an achievable solution? The easiest way to lose a relationship is to try to sell something they do not need or that will not solve their issues. If your product or service cannot address their current issue, assist them in finding an alternative solution. It's an excellent opportunity to show empathy. Can you think of at least six reasons your customer should consider your product or service? If you can think of six, it's potentially a perfect target.

Competitive Advantage

A competitive advantage goes beyond your ability to solve the problem. It's your ability to solve the problem better than your competitors. Do you have a feature that provides a superior benefit? Does your product or service have a marketable advantage over your competition, or is it a unique solution—a solution that only you can provide? You can create an advantage by your desire to provide better service than your competition.

Referrals

Referrals are your best resource for warming a cold call. The average salesperson doesn't use referrals because they don't ask. Customer relationships that grow into trust and friendships will provide referral opportunities. I always ask for referrals and testimonials. Customers often don't want to take the time to write testimonials, so consider offering to write them with their input. It's seamless and practical.

I would not accept a customer's money unless I believed my product could provide an effective solution. I wanted every new potential customer to possess all five characteristics, but their ability to have the budget, and my ability to reach a decision-maker and to solve the problem, are inescapable.

Review Questions

- How would you describe the perfect target customer?
- How do you approach new customers?
- How do you determine if a customer has the budget to purchase your product or service?
- What system do you use to be sure you are speaking with the buying decision-maker?
- How do you ask for referrals?

14

Building Positive Relationships

Every interaction with another person, whether it be someone new or someone you have known for a while, will help build either a positive or negative relationship.

I HAD A teammate whose political beliefs differed from mine. We may never agree on those, but our shared values and shared interests helped build a positive relationship. We were both grounded in strong family values. We were both active in our church, prayed to the same God, and were willing to give our time and resources to those in need. He was the only person on staff with a four-wheel drive vehicle and was everyone's transportation to work during a major snowstorm. We both understood the value of teamwork and enjoyed working together.

How people express disagreements frequently causes more conflict than the disagreement itself.

He was a good person, but we often agreed to disagree. How people express disagreements frequently causes more conflict than the disagreement itself. Reasons for differences can be communicated without attacking someone's character. Building relationships based on shared values and shared interests requires approaching issues with an open mind. It's your willingness to respect opinions that differ from your own.

His political opinions contradicted mine, but we maintained a good working relationship. We understood that to achieve results that would satisfy our company's objectives and our families' needs, it was essential to focus on our company's vision and mission. Winning or losing was a team effort. He was gregarious and skilled at developing good relationships.

Relationships can often mature organically, but are sometimes created with "authentic intentionality." Shared values and shared interests can be more powerful than shared beliefs. Ask questions and seek to discover "shared values." Try not to focus on what divides us but on what values, interests, and purpose we share.

Relationships Built on Friendliness and Kindness

Friendliness and kindness are very powerful attitude characteristics; it takes little if any effort to be kind to someone, no matter the type of relationship. Being truthful and doing what you say you will do is an incredible opportunity to establish or maintain a positive relationship, whether it's with friends, a spouse, work associates, or business partners. Greet everyone with a smile, extend a firm handshake, and maintain eye contact. The saying "You will reap what you sow" reflects the idea that actions have consequences. If you want to be treated with kindness, you should have a kind spirit. It's essential to have a likable personality, regardless of your professional pursuits. Friendliness and kindness are the foundation for being liked, and building positive relationships is rooted in your ability to be likable.

Be likable; keep your promises. Although it may seem like common sense, many people struggle to achieve this straight-forward objective. It is one of the 12 actionable activities mentioned in an upcoming chapter, Finding Your Sweet Spot. Complete what you said you would complete before you said you would complete it.

The most critical time in any relationship, positive or negative, is the first three to six seconds you meet someone. Your ability to have a positive approach will help make relationship-building more seamless. There is nothing more essential during the sales process than being liked. Most customers prefer to do business only with people they like unless the product or ser-vice has an overwhelming competitive advantage. Even in those situations, a customer will drop you as soon as a more likable competitor can effectively satisfy their needs.

Trust

Jim Waits observed my ability to connect with his staff and his family before he invited me to his office. Our relationship grew from a customer/vendor relationship into a customer/ trusted friend relationship. He became a consistent customer and business partner. I created his monthly radio advertising schedule based on his budget, and he never asked for the cost per commercial. He correctly assumed that I would deliver the best rates possible. I had earned his trust.

Earning trust from someone new and without a referral from a trusted friend of your customer requires time. Trust must be cultivated and nurtured. Trust is maintained by honoring commitments, exceeding expectations, and understanding the power of empathy. There is no greater reward than earning the trust of others.

The following are seven steps to help garner trust:

1. Be honest. Integrity is one of a person's most important personality characteristics. Tell the truth no matter what the situation.
2. Be transparent. It helps to create trust and respect.
3. Be eager to exceed expectations. Explore opportunities to under-promise and over-deliver as much as possible.
4. Be recognized as an expert. Make self-improvement a part of your daily strategy.
5. Be referred to by a trusted friend. Have the courage to ask for referrals. They help move relationships from likes to positive relationships quickly.
6. Be willing to create a list of testimonials from recognized sources. Testimonials are a close second to referrals. They are the trophies on the mantelpiece.
7. Be proactive when making a mistake. Mistakes are a part of life. But when you make a mistake, let your customer know immediately.

The Relationship Pyramid

The Relationship Pyramid illustrates the process that leads to trust and friendship. The first two stages make up over two-thirds of the space on the pyramid. Your ability to be liked is the most seamless stage, while friendship is made of the tip—the smallest and most difficult position to occupy.

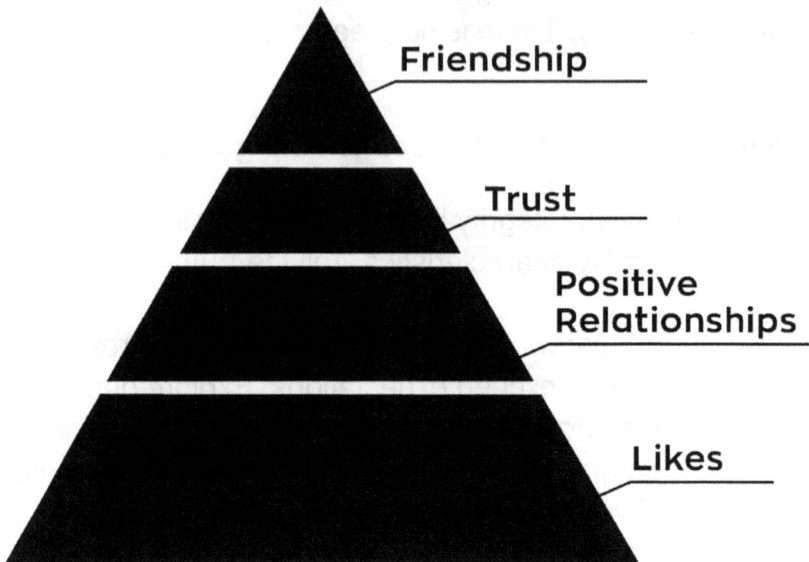

- Stage one: A likable approach. A firm handshake, a genuine smile, and a solid understanding of your customer's business and industry will help you be liked quickly. Making a first impression takes only three to six seconds, and being liked is the foundation of an emotional connection.
- Stage two: A positive relationship starts with an emotional connection that happens during the approach. At this stage, you will begin to identify shared values, interests, and beliefs, enabling your customers to feel at ease when sharing their challenges, issues, aspirations, and objectives.
- Stage three: Building Trust, goes beyond positive relationships. It's when you have exhibited genuine empathy for your customer's current and desired situation, and you have a thorough understanding of whether there is a gap between the two, and the consequences if the gap cannot be narrowed or eliminated. It's when

your customer feels your concern about them and their business beyond a shadow of a doubt, and your meticulous attention to their needs has made you a trusted partner.

- Stage Four: Trust helps build friendships. When you are trusted, your business relationship can evolve into a friendship. This kind of relationship doesn't happen often, but when it does, it makes doing business seamless. When you reach this stage, your customer considers you a valuable member of their team.

Any relationship rooted in trust and friendship has an opportunity to last a lifetime. It's a relationship based on honesty and integrity. You will discover that your customers want you to succeed as much as you want them to succeed. It creates win-win outcomes. Positive relationships are an ingredient of living a positive life. Unless you are isolated on an island, every interaction with another person either starts, supports, or ends a relationship. Whether that relationship is positive or negative is primarily dependent on you.

Review Questions

- How have you used shared values to build relationships?
- Do you consider yourself a likable person, and why?
- What have you done to earn someone's trust?
- What have you done that helped you overcome a bad first impression?
- What have you done that helped you move from likes to friendships?

15

Critical and Creative Thinking

I have discovered that one of the most liberating characteristics anyone can possess is their ability to think critically and creatively.

KEVIN WAS KNOWN for his exceptional wit within the team. He was clever and a quick thinker. He was the person everyone wanted to be involved in their brainstorming sessions. His ability to discern customer challenges and problems was genuinely remarkable. He was a charmer, and everyone had respect for his ability to solve problems, but he was also one who would create a solution that, on occasion, was at his teammates' expense. He used his critical and creative thinking skills to his full advantage. Kevin understood that sales were both an art and a science.

The sales process requires working within a system while using imagination and intuition to solve problems. Critical and creative thinking is the foundation of initiating ideas that no one else has considered possible.

Kevin was customer-focused and could calculate his commission before closing a sale. He was always exploring revenue-generating opportunities that no one else had considered. He had cultivated several strong relationships with auto dealership owners and general managers, and chose to focus on targeting some of these same dealerships. After weeks of market analysis, he noticed that over 30 auto dealers, representing almost every domestic and import automobile, were located on one thoroughfare. He believed it was an excellent opportunity to help create an Automobile Dealers Association.

However, he faced a challenge: Only one of those dealerships was on his account list, so he first had to convince his sales manager that he was creating a new revenue source that wouldn't interfere with his teammates. The next challenge was convincing as many competing dealers as possible to participate in the program. Because the movie *Star Wars* had reached colossal popularity, the radio station's creative team branded the marketing campaign "CAR WAR." Ten dealers agreed to combine a small portion of their monthly advertising budgets to invite potential car buyers from all parts of the metro area to consider purchasing a car from one of their dealerships. Several makes and models were represented. The campaign was very successful and lasted for over a year. The idea won a national award for "out-of-the-box thinking," another phrase used to illustrate critical and creative thinking.

Review Questions

- Do you consider the sales process an art or science, and why?
- Can you share an example of how you use the art of the sales process to your benefit?
- How do you excel in the science of the sales process?
- What are some examples of your ability to think critically?
- Do you consider yourself a creative thinker, and why?

16

The Plan

The more difficult the destinations, the more strategic the plans.

CJ WAS AN excellent salesperson, but struggled to reach his goal of becoming the top revenue-producing salesperson on his team. His spontaneous sales style was both a blessing and a curse. He could wing it better than anyone on staff. CJ's gregarious personality compensated for his lack of preparation. Most people liked him the moment he was introduced. An upbeat personality is critical, but to be the best, you must not only create a plan but also execute it.

CJ required a more hands-on leadership style to help him reach his full potential. It didn't mean he needed to be micromanaged; that approach would likely drive him away. But implementing a system to manage his weaknesses benefited him and the company. His sales manager helped him create daily mini-goals that, when completed, would help him achieve his overall goals and objectives. He also helped CJ to better understand his closing ratio. This gave him a specific number of accounts he needed to reach that would help him achieve his revenue objectives and put him in a position to win every sales award.

CJ was asked to bring a copy of his business plan to every one-on-one meeting with his sales manager. This was the perfect time for him to share his daily accomplishments and focus on the activities that helped him achieve his goals and objectives. It was also a good time to make adjustments if needed. It helped him to be prepared when he was asked to lead one of their sales meetings.

He also understood and effectively implemented the "power of one more" as a consistent tactic—a small extra time investment done daily that delivers incredible results.

CJ recognized that making one extra call daily, five days a week, 48 weeks a year, would help him achieve his goal while increasing his compensation. The results would be 240 extra calls or attempts annually, allowing one vacation week per quarter. A 10 percent closing ratio would result in two new customers per month. If the average value of each customer was $5,000 with a commission rate of 10 percent, his total yearly revenue would increase by $120,000, and his annual income would increase by $12,000.

He aimed to reach one additional customer daily by phone or in person, making it part of his daily routine. This practice also helped him improve his cold- and warm-calling techniques.

Understanding his closing ratio and its impact on his revenue and income motivated him to enhance his ability to develop solutions and presentation skills, which are crucial steps in the sales process. Increasing his closing ratio by 5 percent could increase his annual income by an additional $6,000.

A combination of a more structured plan and his gregarious personality led to success beyond his imagination.

Effective business plans encompass the company's vision, mission, and purpose while establishing goals, strategies, objectives, and tactics that help guide daily activities. They are designed to help you manage your time and prioritize tasks. Creating a plan should be taken seriously and not merely seen as busy work. The quality of your plan will demonstrate your critical and creative thinking abilities as well as the effort you invest in its development. If done correctly, its use will dictate your success. Avoid activities that don't support your goals and objectives. There is a difference between activity and productivity.

Every salesperson and sales manager on staff was required to create a business plan each year. A business plan template was provided to ensure team consistency. It was designed to identify the strategy, objectives, and tactics needed to help achieve the overall company revenue goal. The sales managers' plan was based on the plans they received from each salesperson. The planning process began in early October of the current year, with completion required by the first Monday of December. This gave everyone ample time to create the plan and make necessary adjustments before the new year.

························

There is a difference between activity and productivity.

························

Questions you should ask during the planning process include the following:

- What goals do you want to accomplish?
- How do they satisfy the company's vision, mission, and purpose?
- Are the goals realistic?

- Are they fluid and flexible?
- What strategies/tactics are needed to accomplish each goal?
- Who should be your collaborators?
- What other resources do you need?
- How are the results measured?
- What timelines will be used to keep you on track?
- What are the consequences if your goals are not realized?

Creating goals is also an art and a science. It requires using the sales process while also using your critical and creative thinking skills.

I have experienced occasions when senior leadership presented unrealistic goals. The only thing they accomplished was to hurt productivity. Goals should be challenging yet achievable, and they require careful planning.

One of the most egregious production killers is procrastination. People who wait until tomorrow to do what they could have done today usually never accomplish their goals. Why set a goal if you are not motivated to achieve it within a reasonable timeframe?

Good Plans Are Workable and Adjustable

Your plan serves as your blueprint for success and should be an integral part of your weekly routine, helping you persevere during challenging times. It will help you focus on productive activity. However, you can minimize its value if it sits on a shelf, collects dust, and is not used until the end of the year when you need a template to help create next year's business plan. There might be a need to adjust. Good plans aren't static. They are designed to help keep you on track. But be fluid. Some situations make plan adjustments necessary.

The following situations signal a need to change your current plan:

Changed Market Conditions

Revenue goals are often based on projections and forecasting, especially when the plan is completed before the end of the fourth quarter, and your budgeting process is based on a calendar year. Accurate forecasting helps to create realistic goals. Unexpected events, such as the 2007–09 financial crisis and the COVID-19 pandemic of 2020–23, compelled every business to adjust its business plans. Natural weather disasters such as tornadoes, hurricanes, floods, and wildfires can necessitate adjustments to existing plans. Sometimes the business climate exceeds expectations, and upward adjustments may be necessary.

Changed Technology

Technology changes daily. Whenever a business creates a tool that enhances productivity, it may need to adjust its plan or forecast. There are a number of businesses that help change the business landscape. The music industry's distribution changed from retail to online downloads. The shelf life of technical innovation gets shorter every day.

Changed Decision-Maker

Sometimes the decision-maker changes, and you need to start building a new relationship. Relationships and trust take time. One of my teammates' largest accounts changed advertising agencies, which reduced her influence on the customers' buying decisions. Her revenue forecast had to be adjusted to make her goals more realistic.

Changed Product or Service

There could be a product change. Your customer could decide to add a new product or delete an existing one. Either way, it could affect your relationship with the customer. One of my customers added several new products to their inventory, creating a new opportunity and prompting me to adjust our plan. On another occasion, senior leadership changed the format of one of my radio stations from rock to old school hip-hop, and the station ratings grew by over 30 percent. We quickly upgraded our revenue forecast.

Changed Customer Focus

Remember that customers buy for their reasons, not yours. I've had an experience where a customer stopped advertising without an apparent cause. He never explained, and his business was a significant part of our annual plan. The experience taught me never to be surprised. Hope for the best, but plan for the unexpected.

Review Questions

- How do you create your business plan?
- How is your plan utilized daily?
- What are some of your time management techniques?
- What happens if you are presented with an unrealistic goal?
- What has caused you to need to adjust an exciting business plan?

17

Preparation or Perspiration

Being underprepared is like being underdressed;
people wonder why you're here.

I PLAYED FOOTBALL for the legendary Coach Roy Kidd at Eastern Kentucky University. He instilled in every player the importance of being better prepared than our opponents. It meant embracing activities that others refused to consider. He believed it was always better to be overprepared than underprepared. Coach Kidd's system was so well-prepared that even when opposing coaches knew our plays and strategy, they couldn't stop it. He achieved 16 conference titles, made 17 NCAA Division 1-AA playoff appearances, and is ranked sixth among the all-time winningest coaches in NCAA history with 314 victories.

Dr. Kevin W. Cosby is also one of the most prepared people I have ever known. He is the senior pastor at St. Stephen Baptist Church and president of Simmons College in Louisville, Kentucky. Dr. Cosby has an outline and subject for every weekly service for the upcoming year, which is completed by November of the previous year. His fluid schedule makes it necessary for him to always be prepared for the unexpected.

He became senior pastor at age 20 and grew the membership from 300 to over 10,000 across three campuses in two states. He also helped revive Simmons College, a school founded in 1879, from a single building to 14, added on-campus housing, and expanded the student body from under 50 to over 600. All are examples of his attention to preparation.

As a sales professional and leader, I sought to emulate the best practices of individuals who consistently achieved success when success seemed unattainable. It was a test of my ability to think critically by asking:

- What were the reasons for their success?
- How could I incorporate a few of their abilities without adjusting my style?

The success of the best media sales professionals never depended on ratings. They understood the importance of preparation.

Coach Kidd and Dr. Cosby demonstrate how thorough preparation can significantly reduce anxiety and boost confidence.

Being well-prepared has a calming effect, relieving tension when making a sales presentation.

The phrase "Never let them see you sweat" was launched as a marketing slogan for Gillette in 1984. It illustrates how Gillette razors helped take the stress out of shaving. There are times when sales can cause the same amount of anxiety. But you never need to sweat if you are thoroughly prepared. Success can be as simple as "doing more than expected." Being well-prepared has a calming effect, relieving tension when making a sales presentation.

It's evident to customers if you have taken the time to prepare. Thorough preparation enables you to anticipate and effectively address every customer objection. Be prepared. The Boy Scout motto means that you are always ready to do what is necessary to help others. It also means that you are ready, willing, and able to do what is needed.

Being well-prepared includes an understanding of the following:

Your product or service

Aspire to establish yourself as an authority and expert on how your product or service can benefit your customers. Seek out training opportunities, conduct thorough research, and consult with colleagues and industry experts. Practice, and practice often. Know your strengths, weaknesses, opportunities, and threats.

Your competitive advantage

What differentiates your product and service from those of your competitors? Do you have a competitive advantage? If so, how does it benefit your customers, and how obvious is the advantage to them? Do your solutions meet the primary benefits your customers are seeking? You need a comprehensive understanding of your competition.

Your customer and your customer's industry

Presenting your solutions without a granular understanding of your customer, their business, or their industry is a recipe for disaster. What are your customers' interests? Do your homework. What benefits are your customers and their clients seeking? Being prepared means knowing as much as possible about their product or service. Use every search and social media platform. If applicable, build a rapport with the gatekeeper and conduct in-store surveys at a physical location.

Your customer's problem or challenge

Initiate deep-dive customer needs analysis meetings. Recognize and acknowledge your customers' problems, challenges, needs, and wants. Never assume that you know the answer to any of those questions. In a previous chapter, we mentioned the importance of asking good, open-ended questions.

Your customers' competitors

Who are your customers' primary competitors? Do they have competitive advantages? Can your product give your customers a competitive advantage? Can you leverage a current customer to help your new customer gain a competitive advantage?

Your approach

Your approach can make all the difference. What matters is not what you say but how you say it. Your desire to help your customer win against their competition is what matters. Your ability to exhibit empathy will come to the surface.

Most businesses have a language specific to their industry. Learn how to use their vernacular seamlessly. For example, when an auto dealer says they are working on their "floor plan," they are referring to managing the line of credit used to finance their cars before they are sold to the consumer. What is an "end-cap display" in the grocery business? It is a display at the end of an aisle in the store, often used to promote specific products or promotional opportunities.

Discover which of their products delivers the highest financial returns or helps deliver the most buyer traffic. Are they privately or publicly traded? If publicly traded, what is their price per share of stock, and how are they trending? Is their business seasonal? Do they have a set buying cycle? Who are their top three competitors and how are they ranked? Are they on a calendar year or a fiscal year? Are they located in multiple markets? Do they have numerous locations in your market, and if so, how many? Is there more than one decision-maker? This is excellent information to use during your sales presentation. It shows your customer that you've taken the time to understand their business. It helps create a trusting relationship and is an excellent opportunity to differentiate yourself from competitors.

Being very prepared will also help you during an employment interview. I trained a recent college graduate and shared some of the techniques presented in this book with him. He was the only candidate to show up in a shirt and tie. He was familiar with the interviewer's alma mater, some of their interests, and their background with the company. He used their mission statement in his presentation and asked great open-ended questions. This impressed the interviewer so much that he offered him the job on the spot. You can never be overprepared or overly persistent.

Never Make Assumptions

Preparedness helps to reduce assumptions. During my early years as a sales manager, I would walk through a local bar and grill across the street from our radio station on my way to the office. A man sat at the bar every day, having the same meal: two eggs over easy, toast, bacon, and a cup of coffee. He was casually attired and possessed a warm and welcoming smile. On one occasion I decided to stop and join him for breakfast. It was the start of a great relationship. We shared ideas and stories at least three days a week for several months. One day I told him I was looking to buy a house and needed to talk to someone about financing. He pulled out a business card with the name of a senior VP at a local bank and said, "Give her a call; they've been trying to get my business for years." Little did I know that this guy was worth millions. That was many years ago, and I still do business at the same bank. It was another valuable epiphany: Never make assumptions or judge a book by its cover.

> **Being prepared helps create an emotional connection with your customers.**

Being prepared helps create an emotional connection with your customers. It's your opportunity to display empathy during the sales process, and it distinguishes you from your competitors. This kind of relationship starts with being well-prepared.

Success will make you a target. Successful people will attract good and bad competitors. Be prepared to defend the mountain you have created. Almost every media salesperson in the market monitors competing radio and TV stations to help generate leads. You must prepare your customers for an influx of calls once your competitors hear your ads on the air. They will come from behind after you have done the work of introducing new customers to your platform. It's another reason your ability to build a trusted relationship is important. Growth not only depends on adding new customers, but also on reducing attrition.

Get to know your opponents—your competitors. Understand their strengths, weaknesses, opportunities, and threats. Do they have a competitive advantage? Do they have an aggressive sales team? Avoid using negativity when discussing your competition with your customers. Focus on your strengths and always provide better service. Remember, people buy from people they like. I don't recall completely losing any of my top direct accounts because my competitors were better prepared.

Review Questions

- How do you prepare before you present your ideas to a customer?
- How do you prepare before approaching a new customer?
- When has your preparation helped you move your customer relationship from likes to trust?
- Is there an occasion when you closed a sale because you were better prepared than your competitors? Share details.
- Have you ever missed an opportunity because you were underprepared? If so, what was your strategy moving forward?

18

Practice and Self-Improvement

If you want to be the best that you can be, create time to practice every day. Finding your sweet spot requires a regular regimen of practice.

IMPROVEMENT AND PRACTICE are not mutually exclusive processes. Trying to improve without practice—whether with a teammate, a customer, or yourself—is like fishing without a pole. Role-playing can be an effective tool for practice.

Role-playing with your teammates can be challenging, but it will help you anticipate and effectively respond to customer objections. You can also role-play alone. Stand in front of a mirror and present your ideas. If your solution does not make sense to you, it probably won't make sense to your customer either. Do not present any ideas you are not convinced will help solve your customers' issues.

Do not present any ideas you are not convinced will help solve your customers' issues.

Develop an insatiable desire to improve. Focus on improving one of the eight steps in the sales process daily. Honestly evaluate your strengths and weaknesses. Embellish your strength at every opportunity and manage your weaknesses so they don't become the reason for not reaching your sales sweet spot. You can put yourself in a position to win. Every successful person who has reached their sweet spot, regardless of their occupation or area of interest, has achieved this through hard work and a passion for practice, even when everyone else has taken the day off. Finding your sweet spot isn't easy, and as stated in a previous chapter, there is a reason so few succeed long-term.

Kim and Baiden were allowed to job share, which enabled them to spend more time with their children while maintaining their sales careers. It also allowed them to role-play among themselves before every important sales presentation. One worked every Monday and Wednesday. The other every Tuesday and Thursday, with both working on Fridays. They made a point of pitching many of their most challenging customers on Fridays when they could work together. They became better sales professionals, and their role-playing sessions helped them to better recognize their strengths and weaknesses. Our senior leadership was somewhat skeptical about the process, but it quickly delivered win-win-win results: a win for Kim and Baiden's family, a win for some of our more challenging customers, and a win for the company because it increased their productivity by more than 30 percent.

Always work to reinforce good relationships.

Never take a good customer for granted. Jim Waits had been one of my best customers for several years when a salesperson from a competing radio station persuaded him to switch to their budget for one quarter. Despite Jim's decision to use a competing radio station, I continued to provide services for his business as though nothing had changed. I made myself available to help him and his business whenever he asked. In contrast, the other salesperson rarely made the 35-mile trip to Jim's dealership in Oldham County. After the quarter ended, Jim began including my radio station again, never considering other competitors. Self-improvement also means improving your ability to help your customers. The solutions you create today will always require improvements tomorrow.

Review Questions

- How often do you role-play before sales presentations?
- How often do you practice?
- What are some of your role-playing techniques?
- How often do you enhance the effectiveness of your current solutions?
- How are role-playing sessions used during your weekly one-on-ones?

19

Prospecting

*Adding new customers to your sales pipeline
is like adding fuel to your car.*

STEVE WAS ONE of the most skilled new business developers in the industry. He approached prospecting in the same manner as Tiger Woods approached golf or Michael Jordan approached basketball. It was what he enjoyed. He was tenacious, disciplined, and determined. He prided himself on acquiring new business and never worked fewer than 50 hours weekly. He was willing to invest in networking groups and other sales organizations that would either enhance his skills or provide leads. He was not particularly team-oriented, but management provided a self-contained environment that allowed him to focus entirely on his mission: delivering the best service in the industry while continually seeking out potential customers who could benefit from his assistance. Prospecting was an important part of his business plan.

Steve was different from almost everyone else on his team. He developed his prospecting skills out of necessity. He noticed that most, if not all, of his teammates were handed revenue-producing accounts as a hiring incentive. He was new to the industry, appreciated the opportunity, and quickly recognized that success would require hard work and a comprehensive plan. During a sales meeting, one salesperson jokingly said, "In radio sales, you eat what you kill." Steve thought, *I'm about to lose a few pounds if that's the case.*

If you lack the discipline and determination to make prospecting a part of your business plan, you will never succeed in most sales environments. Prospecting and identifying the perfect customers is the first step in the sales process. A key strategy for mitigating account attrition involves consistently acquiring new customers and integrating them into your sales account pipeline. Before you start prospecting, you must identify the key characteristics of a perfect target customer.

However, Steve knew how to follow his intuition and instincts, effectively utilizing them as valuable tools for prospecting. It can be hard to explain. Intuition can be based on empirical evidence, or simply on a gut feeling. Neither should be ignored. He never dedicated time to customers who didn't meet the characteristics needed to create win-win outcomes.

Steve had a customer who always welcomed him into his office. The customer had multiple locations and appeared to have a large advertising budget. But he would never invest what was needed for a successful radio marketing campaign. Steve finally believed the customer was not being sincere. There was a hidden objection that he couldn't uncover, no matter how many times he asked.

Although it may be necessary to walk away at times, it should never be a permanent solution if the business processes align with the characteristics of the perfect customer. Continue to use every communications platform to reach out about once per quarter. Change is one of the only things in life beyond our control. Never completely bury a customer you are sure you can help.

If a potential customer isn't buying a competitor's product, they're unlikely to buy yours. However, as mentioned before, never judge a book by its cover. Sometimes small-budget customers can become big-budget customers. Almost every large business was once a small business, and you could be the vendor that helps propel them to greatness. Many, if not most, successful businesses started as low-budget operations.

Overcoming objections is not difficult for most experienced salespeople. It can be as simple as asking the proper questions at the appropriate time. Discovering the objection differentiates the average salesperson from the most successful ones. Never assume until you've asked the correct questions. This was discussed in a previous chapter. There were instances when I thought I was speaking to the appropriate decision-maker because he managed the business's day-to-day operations, only to find out later that he did not have the authority to sign the check.

> **Sometimes small-budget customers can become big-budget customers.**

Prospecting requires a well-targeted focus. Avoid the noise around you. Surround yourself with people who encourage you. Don't let your coworkers, family, or friends become distractions. Not everyone will buy into your dream. There are reasons so few people reach their full potential. During Steve's early years in the business, he noticed some team members would spend more time at lunch than prospecting. Prospecting is a lot like practicing; most don't like it, but everyone understands its necessity.

Steve spent hours prospecting. He targeted every competing radio station, TV station, newspaper, billboard, and social media platform. He exuded confidence, believing that every customer in his prospect pipeline would eventually become a revenue-generating customer.

Steve's results were remarkable. He became one of the best media sales professionals in the market. There is an adage that says, "Iron sharpens iron." Resistance will always make you stronger.

Networking Organizations

Join organizations that offer networking opportunities.

But when you join, be an active participant. Attend every meeting, join a committee, and consider becoming an officer. This is an excellent opportunity for your colleagues to observe your work ethic. Remember, information spreads quickly. A reputation will follow you, whether it's good or bad. You'll discover several referral opportunities.

The following is a list of organizations and social media platforms that could help your prospecting effort:

- Local chamber of commerce
- Nonprofit organizations
- Entrepreneurs' organizations
- Business Networking International
- Young Entrepreneur Council
- Rotary clubs
- Social Media groups

Great salespeople are enthusiastic prospectors. They are hunters by nature. They understand that new business development is their business insurance policy. New business developers are very valuable. If you can develop and attract new customers, you will never need to worry about employment opportunities. New business developers do not depend on market conditions to achieve their goals and objectives. They have developed a system/science that is both efficient and effective. They are not merely active, but productive. I have worked with salespeople who always seemed busy but never closed any new business. New business development is often a requirement in most sales environments.

Referrals

Referrals are the next best thing to having a relationship with a target customer.

Jim Waits met every characteristic of a great customer and was a great source of referrals. He referred me to several other auto dealers, many of whom became good customers. Be courageous and always ask for referrals.

Testimonials

While testimonials may not be as impactful as referrals, they remain a valuable prospecting tool. When you have nurtured a positive customer relationship, your customers are likely to agree to either provide a testimonial or allow you to write one on their behalf.

Example of a Testimonial

> This is Bill Smith, owner of Smith's Chrysler Dodge Jeep. I had never considered using the radio in our marketing strategy. We have used newspaper for years and have added various interactive media platforms. We primarily use search and targeting ads on Instagram, Facebook, and Google, all with good results. Jim, my WWWW radio salesperson,

never stopped trying to meet with me. He sent me pertinent information that could help my business every month. Jim's service was better than that of many of my current vendors. This went on for over a year, and I decided to allow him to share his ideas. He discussed the value of a push-pull marketing strategy, suggesting adding radio to the mix to communicate our story to a targeted audience.

After including their station for three months, our business increased by 12 percent, and we can attribute much of the increase to radio. Allow Jim to help you. He's honest and knowledgeable. I am delighted with our results.

Create a list of testimonials. Set a goal of at least 10 to 15. This will impress your potential customers, especially those from well-known businesses.

Review Questions

- What prospecting tool has delivered the best results?
- What is your approach to prospecting?
- What's an assumption that you later discovered was incorrect?
- How do you actively ask for referrals?
- What's an example of a successful testimonial you helped create? Share details.

20

Brand/Position

*When someone makes a descriptive statement
about you or your business, believe them.*

YOLANDA VALUED INTEGRITY and struggled when asked to represent companies whose business practices didn't align with their positioning statement. She was tasked with developing a marketing strategy for an online retailer struggling to fulfill its promises to existing customers. The request included creating a slogan that would completely misrepresent the service their customers were experiencing. She told the owner that a better marketing strategy could not solve their problem. Their problem had everything to do with their operations. She candidly asked the owner, "Why would you invite new customers to use your service if honoring your commitment to your current customers seems challenging?" Yolanda's honesty cost her a financial opportunity, but her impeccable reputation was far more valuable.

The mental picture that comes to mind whenever the name of a product or service is communicated is an illustration of its brand and position. Your brand defines your current identity, and your position is what you do and how it benefits your target customers. It is how you rank among your competitors in the consumer's mind. It's your differentiator. When someone asks about Chick-fil-A, the first thing that comes to mind for most people is exceptional customer service with a friendly smile. That's a significant aspect of their market position.

The cost of including my radio stations in a customer's marketing strategy was double that of every competitor in the market. Both my stations had unique value propositions. Because of their perceived value and market position, the advertising community expected to pay more per commercial. One of the stations shared call letters with one of the market's most dominant television stations, which also helped the station's brand and market position. Potential customers would take our phone calls because of the station's heritage and format dominance.

Understanding how your product or service is valued from your customer's perspective is crucial before you can start designing solutions. Make the following question part of your initial customer interaction.

Example question: *When considering my product or service, what's the first thing that comes to mind?* This is a great question, and it will help you quickly understand your brand and position from your customers' perspective.

We operate in an ever-changing business environment, and your position can change for the better or worse for the same reasons you might need to adjust your strategic plan, as mentioned in an earlier chapter.

In 2004, Blockbuster Video had 9,000 stores valued at $3 billion. The industry changed from DVD rentals to streaming-based subscriptions—an example of how technology can change your market position seemingly overnight. In December 2024, Netflix was trading at $920 per share, valued at over $393 billion. This exemplifies how a leadership vision can shape a company's brand and position.

Elevator Speech

Your company's brand and position in the market should enable you to craft an effective elevator speech. It should include:

- Your product's position
- Your product's value proposition
- Your product's proposed solutions

Example: "Hello, my name is Bill Smith. I've been given the awesome responsibility of representing the top adult-rated radio station in the market. My team and I have created marketing campaigns that have helped several businesses, many like yours, increase their market share—some by double digits. Sharing a few successful testimonials would require approximately 15 minutes. Is there a day of the week and time that works best for you?"

Emotionally Connected Customers

Your brand and position should help create emotionally connected customers. Most every business that experiences long-term success has emotionally connected customers. It's the reason that well-branded products can charge higher prices compared to generic-branded products that sell a similar product.

A brand and position that creates emotionally connected customers can answer the questions below.

Do your product benefits/services meet or exceed customer expectations?

This requires an understanding of all the benefits your customers are seeking. Every company with emotionally connected customers has effectively turned its unique features into customer benefits. You should also recognize the level of importance of each benefit.

Does your company's positioning statement reflect its position?

It's an example of your walk speaking as loudly as your talk. Avoid making difficult promises. Bad business experiences multiply very quickly. Maintaining your position requires continual updates and self-evaluation.

Does your company's mission statement reflect its actual values?

How often have you seen a company's mission statement in full display that is not an accurate representation of their business practices? They claim to be customer-focused but are difficult to reach when issues arise. Or they aim to deliver exceptional value but prioritize profits over customer service. Your core values should be an integral part of your mission statement. Success is achieved when your expressed values align with your demonstrated actions.

Do your beliefs and values reflect your company's values?

The values of the company you represent should support your personal beliefs and values. It's challenging to represent a product that you don't believe in. Sales success requires a level of passion. You will only be passionate about a product or service that can help your customers achieve their goals.

How is your company perceived from your competitor's perspective?

How much do your competitors respect your product or service? Do they view you as good competition? Do their features do a better job of satisfying the benefits sought by your customers? Who has the largest share, and why? Do you have a marketable competitive advantage?

What is your leader's leadership style?

Do you have a good leader? This question can be somewhat subjective. Does your leadership value your opinions? Do they have an open-door policy? Are they willing participants when you are trying to create solutions for your customers? Are they respected in the industry? Treating people with kindness is difficult if you are not being led with kindness.

Do you have a "Fierce Urgency of Now"?

Procrastination is a momentum killer. Don't put off tasks you can complete today until tomorrow. Possessing a "Fierce Urgency of Now" helps you differentiate yourself from your teammates and the competition. It's a quote from Martin Luther King Jr. that, in part, said, "In this unfolding conundrum of life and history, there is such a thing as being too late."

The radio station was a recognized brand and positioned as one of the top-rated radio stations in America. Its position helped open a variety of customers' doors. Country music was king, and we were the only station in the market programming contemporary country music. Country music fans were some of the most loyal in the market. If they liked country music, they listened to our radio station. Its top rating also helped overcome the perception that country music listeners had limited disposable income. It was the furthest thing from the truth. Our listeners were emotionally connected to the radio station.

Review Questions

- What is your company's brand in the market?
- What is your company's position in the market?
- What features does your product or service possess that benefit your customers?
- Have you created an elevator speech? If so, share it.
- How are you creating emotionally connected customers?

21

Persistence

Resistance creates the need for persistence.

If I were to choose between a highly persistent individual with B- intelligence and a highly intelligent individual with B- persistence to join my sales team, high persistence would always prevail.

CHRIS HAD BEEN the radio station's sales manager for several years, and he and his team had created a great workplace culture and reputation. The sales team was generally happy, and recruiting new talent for his sales team was a seamless process. Senior leadership and Chris decided to add a new sales position. Seven people were on the sales team, but revenue was growing so fast that they needed to add new sales professionals. After interviewing several candidates, he hired someone he felt could excel in developing new business.

A week later, Chris began receiving calls from someone seeking an opportunity to interview for a sales position. He had sales experience in a different industry; however, Chris had just hired the candidate he believed to be the best fit for the position. The candidate called at least three times a day for three consistent days. Chris's sales assistant told him the position had been filled, but he wouldn't stop. One day someone slid an envelope under the door while he was in the men's room. It contained the candidates' resume. His persistence sparked his curiosity. *Who is this person who refuses to give up?* Obviously, courage was not an issue. Chris finally gave him an interview; it was one of the best he had experienced in his sales leadership career.

Chris asked human resources to conduct a background check and went to senior leadership to secure the funding to add him to the team. He soon became one of their station's most outstanding new business developers. He earned over $100,000 during his second full year on staff. He persistently sought meetings with some of the most challenging customers. He had a knack for being persistent without being annoying. He had a unique ability to connect with gatekeepers. He proved to be competent, confident, courageous, and a person of high character. He would not have had the opportunity if he had given up too quickly. Persistence is the universal characteristic that every successful self-made person possesses.

Most of the time, persistence is the primary difference between success and failure. You may not win them all, but never because you gave up too soon. Many of my customers said, "You refuse to give up. How many times must I say no?" My response was always, "Yes, you are correct. I don't give up when I believe I can help someone solve their issues and challenges better than my competition." Don't you want your sales team to have the same belief while representing your product?

During my early years as a member of a radio sales team, one of our top customer prospects was a retailer who used radio as their primary marketing platform. The owner did not consider including my station in the advertising mix. He used another radio station whose target audience demographic did not match the demographic of his primary customer. Most of his customers were women between the ages of 35 and 64, and the station he used had a target audience of men aged 50 and above. The customer chose his favorite station over one that could reach a higher percentage of his potential customers. My station had twice the number of female listeners aged 35 to 64 than all the other stations in the market. I supplied market and industry information and provided weekly station features that could benefit the business. I would stop by his stores unannounced to do in-store surveys. I knew the cashiers and store managers by name. I was always prepared with an idea whenever I walked into his store.

One day I was invited to his office without notice, and he wanted to hear what we had to offer. I told him it was more important for him to share some of his challenges so that I could create solutions based on his needs. After days of developing new ideas, I returned to his office with what I believed would increase his market share. However, he was still sold on the other station until I took a mirror from my briefcase and asked him to look at it. He wondered why, and I told him I had a reason. Remember, he had chosen his favorite radio station. I asked if his reflection in the mirror represented the demographic of most of his customers. He could only say no and agreed to use my radio station for one quarter. The results were incredible, and my radio station became an important part of his marketing strategy for several years.

There is no quality more important for sustainable success than persistence. A small percentage of people achieve their full potential because they lack the willpower to be persistent. Persistence is the quality that motivates and inspires someone to continue despite resistance. It can come from various directions. Most people do not recognize the cost of their inability to remain committed. All notable accomplishments were preceded by difficulty. The opposite of persistence is surrender.

Never surrender if you believe in yourself and your product or service. Never allow anyone to tell you what you can or cannot accomplish. And never stop telling yourself encouraging stories.

According to studies, 50 percent of salespeople give up after the first call, and less than 5 percent make it past the fifth call. It is widely believed that more than 10 attempts are required to successfully reach a new customer. Never give up; situations will change, and persistence can help you be in the right place at the right time.

And never stop telling yourself encouraging stories.

While servicing my Radcliff and Elizabethtown, Kentucky, customers, I visited every new car dealership in the area. Every owner or general manager welcomed me to their office, including those who rarely used the station. On one of those occasions, I happened to stop by a dealership that had received funding from its corporate leadership to incorporate radio into its marketing strategy. Being in the right place at the right time was a significant win for the station and the dealership.

Review Questions

- How would you rate your level of persistence from 1 to 10, and why?
- When did your persistence create a sales opportunity? Give details.
- Have you ever given up on a perfect customer? If so, why?
- When were you at the right place and time because of your persistence? Share examples.
- Have you ever been bothered by someone else's persistence? If so, how did you react?

22

Presentation

Your presentation is an invitation to build a relationship.

THE PHRASE "LIGHTS, camera, action" is commonly used to signal the beginning of an event or activity. This marks when all prior steps have been completed, and the final product is ready to be presented. The presentation provides an up-to-date snapshot of your ability to identify and understand your customers' challenges and issues. It's your opportunity to display your critical and creative thinking skills. You have qualified and approached the customer with a valid value proposition, conducted a thorough needs analysis, and created a solution-based proposal. Now it's time to present your ideas. The ability to present your ideas effectively is the fifth step in the sales process.

Kinley had been a sales team member for less than two years but became an outstanding presenter. She meticulously followed the sales process. She demonstrated strong organizational skills and attention to detail. She took the time to role-play before all her sales presentations to help her anticipate objections before every meeting. She sought ideas from her teammates during sales meetings and her sales manager during one-on-one sessions. She enjoyed generating innovative ideas, particularly when she was confident that her solutions were superior to those of the competition. She never presented an idea without an alternative solution, which happened to be another technique she used to anticipate objections. Her customers loved her because of her active listening skills. She made an effort to do less than 25 percent of the talking and understood the power of silence. Her ability to trial close during the presentation was so seamless that it went unnoticed. Kinley took full advantage of the opportunity to move her positive customer relationships to the next step of the Relationship Pyramid: Trust.

Talking vs. Listening

As a presenter, you must have good vocal and listening skills, but the most important thing is to incorporate purposeful listening into your strategy. You will never become a successful salesperson by talking more than your customer. This is a problem for a large percentage of traditional salespeople. They focus on their product or service rather than analyzing customer needs and fostering positive relationships.

Some salespeople work hard to secure an opportunity to present, only to squander it by failing to focus on the most important thing: discovering their customers' needs.

Purposeful listening skills do not happen naturally. It requires training. Many individuals assume they are effective listeners, yet often they listen with the intent to respond rather than to understand.

Purposeful listeners fully concentrate, understand, respond, and remember what is said. It's also another opportunity to display empathy for your customers.

Body Language

Body language speaks louder than words. Customers can perceive your empathy and confidence through your body language and posture. Lean forward slightly when your customer is speaking, and nod to show that you understand when applicable. Present a genuine smile, maintain eye contact, and never sit with your arms crossed during a sales presentation. It's also essential to keep a keen eye on your customers' body language during an in-person sales presentation. Are they helping to make eye contact? Are they looking at their computer or allowing interruptions, such as taking phone calls, while you are presenting? Do they have their arms crossed? Or are they capturing every word, slightly leaning forward, and answering and asking good questions? Are you asking questions that help the customer stay engaged? If their body language suggests a lack of interest, it might be a great time to try a trial close. It's appropriate to ask if your proposed solutions are on point.

The Power of Silence

Be aware of asking questions in a manner that gives your customer a sense of question overload. Golden Silence, developed by Miller Heiman, is a reliable technique that makes asking questions both seamless and an effective negotiating tactic. Pause for at least three to four seconds after your customer answers each question before asking the next one, when applicable. Never answer the questions that you ask while presenting to a customer during negotiation. Don't be the person who makes the first concession. People often become uncomfortable during silence and feel compelled to respond first.

Silence is Golden

The phrase "Speech is silver, silence is golden" is believed to have originated in Arabic culture as early as the ninth century, but was coined by poet Thomas Carlyle in 1831, according to Wikipedia. Silence is powerful because of its ability to make a person uncomfortable.

I was purchasing a car several years ago and felt my trade-in was worth an additional $500. I presented the check for the purchase, $500 less than the asking price, and remained silent. The dealer noticed the discrepancy, and I remained silent. I had a car, my trade-in, and a check in my hand. It was up to the dealer whether to close the deal. It worked, and I drove off the lot in a new car. Silence is golden when used strategically.

> **Trial closing is your sales presentation temperature gauge.**

Never interrupt your customers while they are answering questions and sharing information. You could cause your customers to stop talking when they were about to share the most critical information needed to help address their issues.

Silence is a very effective presentation and communication tool.

Trial Closing

Trial closing is a great tool to help uncover objections. It is a technique that enables you to stay on the correct path. It helps ensure clarity at every stage of your sales presentation. Trial closing is your sales presentation temperature gauge. Tackling objections during the presentation becomes more seamless, thereby enhancing customer engagement. It helps you become a *purposeful listener instead of a talking presenter*. Effective trial closing can make the closing process a natural part of the presentation. Closing also becomes seamless. There are times when objections are no more than misunderstandings.

The difference between a closing statement and a trial closing statement is that a closing statement asks for a decision, whereas a trial closing statement asks for an opinion.

Written Presentations

Written presentations can significantly impact your chances of successfully closing a sale. I worked with a salesperson whose written sales presentations included a variety of colors and 12-letter words when 6-letter words would have been sufficient—especially when he didn't understand their correct meaning and rarely, if ever, corrected his spelling. His ideas were never considered, due to a poorly written proposal or presentation.

Bigger is not necessarily better. Be concise and comprehensive.

Your written proposal is a tangible reflection of yourself. If done poorly, it's like attending a formal dinner in jeans and a T-shirt.

Your chances of closing grow once you reach the presentation stage of the sales process. It is now time for you to explain how your proposed solution will yield the best results. A strategy that always increases your chances of closing is to offer multiple solutions. For instance, if you provided three solutions while each of your three competitors offered one, the customer would typically evaluate which of your three options could yield the best possible outcome before considering the other three, and significantly improve your chance of earning their business. This is another excellent opportunity to differentiate yourself from your competitors.

There is truth in the old saying, "Customers don't care what you know until they know you care."

Review Questions

- How would you rate your ability to trial close, and why?
- What have you done to be a better listener?
- When were you able to positively gauge a customer's body language? Share details.
- Can you share an occasion when the power of silence would have been a benefit?
- What strategy do you use when preparing for a sales presentation?

23

Personality

Your positive personality will build positive partnerships.

GEORGE WAS A very likable sales team member and got along well with almost everyone he met. His ability to connect with everyone set him apart from the competition and his teammates. His smile could light up a room. He never seemed to have a bad day. He wasn't very organized, but he did a great job utilizing all his resources to help him meet his deadlines. Sales assistants went out of their way to help him because of his pleasant personality. He invited one of his customers every Friday for happy hour and played golf with customers whenever they were available. He was also the life of the party, always finding reasons to celebrate.

John was just the opposite of George. John was somewhat introverted, didn't like crowds, and usually stayed alone, interacting little with his teammates. He was very structured and organized. He crossed every T and dotted every I, and made a point of thoroughly understanding his customers. John knew their birthdays and never missed sending cards and gifts on holidays. He was pleasant but subdued. Most of his customers liked his no-nonsense approach to solving their needs and challenges. He would rather read a book or periodical about one of his customers' industries than go out for drinks. He made providing unequaled service a part of his everyday routine.

Who do you believe was the most successful sales professional? They were both top performers, highly competitive and aware of their rankings among their teammates. Both could be relied upon if a final effort was needed to meet their monthly sales target. The reality is, they were both excellent salespeople, each taking full advantage of their unique strengths.

Whether you are an extrovert or introvert, laid-back or aggressive, creative or uninspired, trustworthy or deceptive, courageous or fearful, empathic or apathetic, these characteristics determine your approach to interacting with different people.

It begins with recognizing the characteristics that make you who you are. As Michael Jackson said, it starts with the "Man in the Mirror." Your ability to identify different personalities is essential to successful problem-solving.

The stories about George and John illustrate the fact that no single personality is required for you to become a successful sales professional. I have seen successful salespeople who were highly gregarious and others who were somewhat introverted, but all were likable, empathic, and possessed the four C-word characteristics.

Are you in control of your emotions, or do your emotions control you? How would you react if there were more days in a month than dollars in your bank account, or if your commissions exceed expectations? Or if a customer repeatedly declined your proposed solutions over several months?

Use challenging times to help define who you are. Remember iron sharpens iron. Resistance builds muscle. These are the times when your competitive personality should come to the surface. Additionally, don't allow your success to take away your edge. Do not internalize all the positive recognition you may be receiving and start to take success for granted. Success can be inspiring, but it can also make you comfortable. Comfort is an enemy of sustained success. It can happen gradually, without you realizing you have moved away from many activities that once made you successful. George and John had different styles based on their personality, but both were very competitive. They were winners and never liked to appear to be losing. They were the kind of people who gave senior leadership confidence that they could overcome almost any challenge.

Engaging with customers effectively requires a comprehensive understanding of their personalities. Some customers made negotiating rates a game of winning at all costs. That experience was shared in a previous chapter.

••••••••••••••••••••••••••••••••

**Comfort is an enemy
of sustained success.**

••••••••••••••••••••••••••••••••

Customers are no different from anyone else. Some are extroverted and gregarious, and some are introverted and reserved. Successful customer engagement is more seamless if you can recognize their personalities.

An inviting personality will help create a positive relationship, whether you are more reserved or outgoing. People usually buy from people they like.

High emotional intelligence will help in every endeavor. Emotional intelligence is an awareness of yourself and how you react in different situations. Can you control your emotions when you are facing difficulty? Can you sense someone else's emotional response with level-headedness? Do you know what motivates you? Are external factors needed for you to be motivated to exceed expectations? And can you sense how others are motivated? Can you show empathy for someone else's situation and excel in a social setting? All will illustrate your emotional intelligence.

Your personality can influence your attitude. George and John had different personalities, but they both had great attitudes. Their sales styles did not dictate how they cared for their customers. They took responsibility for their current situation and realized that circumstances were not equal. They chose to work hard rather than blame others for the problems they experienced. It had everything to do with their attitude. Are you a person who always looks for excuses, or are you a person who can find the best in bad situations? As noted, other people can influence your attitude and the narratives you believe about yourself, both positively and negatively.

A positive personality will help you see the best in others while navigating difficult circumstances and focusing on the end, not the present. People with a positive personality do not allow stress to influence their behavior. Remarkable things happen if you have the right attitude coupled with a positive personality. Positive people are optimistic, happy, and joyful. It shows up in their body language and determines how quickly they connect with people they don't know. People are naturally drawn to those with an inviting personality and a positive attitude. Who are the people in your life who always greet you with a smile? They rarely, if ever, have something negative to say about anybody or any situation. They view life from a positive perspective. Guess what? Most customers like those types of people as well.

Happiness is a choice. It's totally up to you.

Review Questions

- How does your personality influence the people around you?
- How accurately do you assess a customer's personality?
- When did your positive personality help create a trusting relationship? Share details.
- How would you rate your emotional intelligence?
- Can you share an example of a time your personality helped you overcome a challenge?

24

Perseverance

Perseverance and persistence are interdependent characteristics.
Those with the discipline to persist also have the
toughness to persevere.

DEMI HAD A good team, and every person was a solid contributor. She understood each person's strengths and weaknesses, and effectively put the right person in the right seat at the right time.

Terry was one of those people. He understood and followed the sales process as well as anyone on the team. He was the salesperson who didn't need to be the top revenue producer, but took pride in achieving all his sales goals and objectives. Terry's results were consistent until three of his top revenue-producing accounts canceled their contracts for reasons beyond his control. Within one week, his year-end sales forecast dropped from 105 percent to less than 75 percent. He was devastated. His usual, somewhat upbeat personality became reserved, and he wore defeat on his sleeve. This was the moment when he would sink or swim—a time to prove his resolve.

Demi encouraged him not to focus on the cancellations, but to concentrate on the activity that had put him in a winning position for months. This was the perfect opportunity to use this setback as a setup for a comeback.

He was encouraged to spend time with his encouragers, the people in his life who possessed a positive personality. He was also advised to facilitate brainstorming sessions with his teammates and customers, set achievable mini-goals to advance him toward success, adjust his account focus, target different customer categories, maintain confidence, and keep the faith. The power that helped him succeed over the years had not abandoned him.

Sales careers can be highly rewarding, but your ability to persevere during challenging times will significantly impact your long-term success. Only a small percentage of new business development radio salespeople survive in the industry for more than a few years. It requires discipline to follow the sales process. Your ability to persevere greatly depends on your character, courage, and commitment. Problems are only as significant as your perception of their outcome—negative or positive. Problems and difficulties are like mountains you face on your way to a desired destination. But every mountain you climb will give you the stamina to climb the next mountain.

Perseverance is a self-belief indicator. It helps to ignite your confidence. Giving up is admitting you don't have what it takes to succeed.

Every outstanding accomplishment was achieved despite challenges, so plan for difficult times. If you have an action plan, you'd better plan to act. Don't dwell on your problems. Worrying only causes high blood pressure and has never been proven to solve a problem. Wins and losses only last for a while. Remember, this will not be the first or last time a mountain has tried to block your path to your destination. See it over, see it around, or see it through.

Persevering through tough times is easier if you recognize those times as a part of life and use the following six perseverance techniques:

1. Visit an Encourager

These are the people who always greet you with a smile. They can come from various sources: family, teachers, religious leaders, customers, or friends. They give you positive reinforcement and are often inspiring nurturers. Sometimes I would make a service call to see a satisfied customer—one who was achieving great results with my product and service. It was an up-to-date testimony about the results that my recommendations could deliver. Make a list of people who are genuinely happy when they see you, and ask yourself why. Write down their reasons and make them *your* reasons. Then believe them.

2. Conduct Brainstorming Sessions

Facilitate a brainstorming session designed to generate new ideas. Participants can include teammates, networking groups, friends and family, and often customers. Every idea should be considered, no matter how far out of the box. Allow freewheeling without judgment or interruption. This is an excellent opportunity to use your critical and creative thinking skills. If properly executed, they can be both fun and effective.

3. Create Mini-Goals

Set additional short-term goals that will support your long-term objectives. These goals should not be a stretch to achieve and are designed to give you a sense of accomplishment. Record each goal on paper and mark them off once completed—at least three and no more than five per day.

4. Trust and Adjust

There will be times when you need to trust your instincts. Instinct and intuition are both important components of *grit*. Revisit your plan and determine whether an adjustment to your vision, mission, or purpose is necessary. Reevaluate your destination. Are your goals and objectives still attainable? Explore new sources of revenue or new and diverse product categories. Don't be afraid to take a detour to get to your final destination.

5. Reevaluate Your Motives

What can you excel at? Achieving this requires a comprehensive understanding of your strengths and weaknesses. Do you possess the competence, confidence, and courage to tackle unforeseen challenges? Giving up may indicate that your goals were not prioritized or that you lacked the grit necessary for success.

Grit has various definitions depending on the author. Those with grit naturally view problems as opportunities for growth. They recognize that their success is linked to identifying and addressing people's issues and challenges. They remain focused and possess a high degree of emotional intelligence. They prefer to surround themselves with others who share their grit, while those lacking it typically prefer to avoid their company. They only respect strong leaders and will assert themselves if they perceive weakness in their leadership.

6. Recognize the Power of Faith

Faith is the strongest path to perseverance. Faith involves believing in something you cannot see. It's your ability and instinct to follow something you don't understand, along with the determination to keep going when you don't feel like it.

It's unexplainable. It's when you know beyond a shadow of a doubt that tough times will not win against tough people.

> *"Now faith is confidence in what we hope for and assurance about what we do not see."*
>
> —Hebrews 11:1

Terry snapped out of his self-pity and used all the techniques he had been taught to overcome adversity. He persevered and finished the year at 97 percent, just short of his yearly revenue objective, but his new strategy gave him a head start for the following year. His latest goal is to challenge all his teammates and become the top revenue producer on the team.

Review Questions

- How do you handle adversity?
- Can you share details of a time it was necessary to adjust your strategy?
- What did you do to overcome an unanticipated obstacle?
- What made you hang in when success seemed impossible?
- What are your examples of using grit?

25

Passion

Passion makes it perfect.

JoEllen was a crucial member of our operations team, taking on several key responsibilities, including business manager, accounts receivable director, assistant traffic director, and occasionally, gatekeeper. She was a highly valued member of our team. JoEllen consistently excelled in her tasks, but her remarkable ability to help collect our receivables stood out. She had a passion for collecting money. Her exceptional talent was evident in the fact that our group of radio stations maintained the lowest outstanding debt among all radio station groups within our company—a point of pride for her. She held monthly one-on-one meetings with every sales team member and assisted them in developing collection strategies as needed. This was an incredible asset for our team. They were compensated based on billing, but would lose commissions if their invoices were not paid within 90 days. JoEllen's emotional connection to the team fueled her passion for collecting receivables. She later became the director of receivables for the entire company. In this role, she led a group of business directors and coordinators, aiding over 100 sales professionals in maintaining their receivable percentage well below industry standards.

Passion is the essential element that connects all the qualities necessary for success in every profession. The most successful sales professionals are passionate about helping customers solve problems and achieve their goals. They are also dedicated to building relationships beyond sales transactions and creating win-win outcomes. Loving what you do reduces the possibility of failure and the challenges of finding another job. It's the difference between having a job and having a career. Sales success is both an art and a science, combining imagination with structure. Your success relies on your customers' success. Customers can sense your empathy, compassion, and passion. All three characteristics help you build trust and friendships. Passion fosters an emotional connection with your customers. Passionate and enthusiastic individuals are a joy to be around; they are the life of the party and the team. They can drop in on customers almost anytime and get an audience unannounced.

Passion can be illustrated in several ways, depending on your sales style. You can be passionate based on your strengths, whether you are a gregarious person or more laid-back. Make it a goal to mirror your customer's passion for their business while adhering to the sales process.

Passion can be cultivated. I knew little about the broadcast sales industry, but I developed a passion for it, which ignited my desire to help people and their businesses. My enthusiasm grew as my customers experienced remarkable success thanks to my recommendations. I was eager to brainstorm with my customers to help them devise marketing strategies and took pleasure in their achievements. They didn't buy every idea, but they considered each one.

Your passion will reflect your purpose, beliefs, and values. All three can unleash your passion and deliver outstanding results.

I have discovered that passion and enthusiasm are both very contagious. If you examine the DNA of most successful people who started with only dreams, the one characteristic they all possess is a passion for what they do. They are sweet spot seekers and enjoy the journey.

Review Questions

- What are the things that ignite your passion?
- Do you love what you do? If so, why?
- What are the ways that you have converted your passion into achievement?
- In what way does your passion reflect your purpose, beliefs, and values?
- Who in your life lives with enthusiastic passion?

Part Two

26

Sales Leadership

"The world is crying out for leaders who build up and not tear down, nurture and not exploit, support and enhance rather than dominate."

—Laurie Beth Jones

DURING MY 29-YEAR sales leadership career, few words have been more powerful or have had as many applications as the word "right." It can be used as a noun, verb, adverb, or adjective. However, a succinct difference exists between being right and doing the right thing. Successful leaders are self-aware and don't need to "be right" all the time. I understood that there were times when following rather than leading provided the best solution—the characteristic of a servant leader. Believe it or not, nobody is always right. Additionally, though it was subjective, I've always tried to do what's right. It's incredible how it makes you feel and helps to create a positive work culture.

What motivates a person to become a sales director or manager? Why would you want to be responsible for the activities of a group of sales professionals with diverse personalities and motivations, as well as increasing the value of the investment made by stakeholders? Balancing "what's right" for your staff, senior leadership, and investors is what makes sales leadership complex.

It requires mastering the ability to lead and manage the day-to-day activities of your sales staff while aligning with the goals and objectives of your company's vision, mission, and purpose. Sales leaders are responsible for recruiting, evaluating, and retaining talent. The best leaders incorporate an inspiring and collaborative leadership style. They also excel at:

- Building a team
- Developing a vision
- Creating a productive culture
- Taking responsibility
- Coaching/nurturing
- Maintaining a positive attitude
- Infusing strong beliefs and willpower
- Communicating continuously
- Building trust
- Displaying authenticity
- Possessing uncompromising integrity
- Exhibiting fearless humility

When I accepted the opportunity to join a radio station sales team, I never considered the possibility of becoming its sales manager. It was a new industry that required my full commitment to survive. The sales staff consisted of several experienced sales professionals, many of whom had previously worked at lower-rated radio stations before being given the opportunity to represent our radio station—the top adult-rated station in the market. They always seemed to have the correct response to every question. I took advantage of every opportunity to listen and to learn how they interacted with their customers.

I also observed the characteristics that made them success-ful and believed I could deliver results as good as, or better than, theirs. It was an opportunity to live a lifestyle beyond my imagination—another example of a valuable epiphany. I incor-porated many of their ideas while maintaining my style.

After 18 months on staff, the general sales manager oppor-tunity at our sister station became available. Their current general sales manager had been promoted to vice president and general manager, and my sales manager suggested that I apply for the job. I had closed several new accounts, and she said it would be a good experience. She felt I had exhibited good leadership qualities.

I prepared a written presentation and pitched for the job. My presentation exceeded their expectations, though I didn't make the finalist list. I realized that getting that job had been a long shot at best, but the experience convinced me that I could be a good radio station sales manager. My focus immediately shifted, and I began to explore the characteristics of great sales leadership as well as those of a successful sales professional.

Several years later, the sales manager position became avail-able at my current radio station. It was the opportunity that I had prepared for over four years. During the interview, I asked the interviewer many of the same open-ended questions I had asked my customers for the past six years. One of my favorite interview questions was "What are the characteristics of the ideal candidate for the opportunity?" There are several more creative ways to ask this question. Set it up with a statement that every interviewer will answer similarly. Creative exam-ple: "I realize staffing is probably the most critical task of any leader. Would you agree? What characteristics would be the most important if you could create the ideal person for this job, and why?" My other favorite question: "What makes this company a good place to work?" Many of my following questions were based on the interviewer's answers. These two simple questions help you to mostly talk about what's important to the interviewer.

I shared my vision for the first week, month, quarter, six months, first year, and five years. It was an example of the adage, "when preparation meets opportunity." Don't wait for an opportunity to present itself. I had a mental picture of what I would do if given an opportunity long before it was available. I believed that I would be a great sales leader and earned the chance to lead our sales team. Most consider the possibility unlikely. But the improbable can be achieved with hard work, purpose, focus, and faith in God.

27

Leadership Myth

IT'S A MYTH that some people are born great leaders. Becoming an effective sales leader requires a combination of coaching, training, emotional intelligence, honesty, integrity, humility, strong communication skills, and on-the-job experience. Recognizing how making unpopular decisions is a natural part of leadership is also essential. A leader's responsibility is to create a vision that their team will follow. Your ability to perform a job well does not guarantee you will be a good leader.

Successful salespeople don't always make successful sales leaders.

Successful salespeople don't always make successful sales leaders. It's challenging for some people to transition from "me" to "we." It requires a complete mindset change from what strategy is good for you to what is good for the team. Promoting your top salesperson to sales manager can be a mistake without a personality assessment or proper training. Sales leaders must recognize that their sales style may differ from many of their team members. No singular style is required.

The first questions every leader should ask themselves each morning:

- What are my team's strengths?
- How can I take advantage of our team's strengths?
- How can I improve our team's weaknesses?
- What can I do to make every person on the team better today than yesterday?
- How should I address today's team challenges?
- What can I do to be a better leader?

28

Staffing

*Evaluating, recruiting, and retaining talent is the
first mission of successful leadership.*

MY BROADCAST SALES leadership career spanned over three
decades, representing a variety of radio formats. Most of my
teams were successful, with some achieving remarkable success. I could attract and retain talented individuals. I sought to
recruit sales professionals who had demonstrated high integrity
and a successful sales background—high-character individuals who possessed courage, confidence, and competence,
and who worked to continually improve their performance and
adhere to the sales process. Minimizing talent attrition and
recruiting are two of the most important leadership tasks.

My first 10 years as a radio station sales leader were incredible.
I inherited a strong sales team that included several tenured
and highly skilled sales professionals. However, my start presented an immediate challenge. I had been a team member for
over five years before being promoted to sales manager. My
fellow team members were aware that I was interviewing for
the sales manager position and witnessed my sales achievements. The transition was somewhat seamless. We were a
cohesive team with minimal personality conflicts, and I had a

good relationship with the entire staff, including our on-air per-sonalities and the production, promotions, and administration teams. Based on their initial response, many were surprised when I was hired, but were willing to give me a chance.

I was confident I had the staff to achieve excellent results. Every person on the sales team had the talent and desire to achieve their individual and station revenue objectives. Garth Brooks gained popularity, and country music became a more mainstream format. This helped further increase the ratings of our highly rated radio station.

Talent evaluation is another part of the staffing process. Analyze each team member's strengths, weaknesses, oppor-tunities, and threats objectively. What are their motivations? What are their individual strengths, weaknesses, opportunities, and threats? Are the team's strengths greater than the team's weaknesses? What are the immediate and long-term threats? Are there opportunities that the previous sales manager didn't recognize? How difficult would it be for every team member to execute the company's vision, mission, and purpose? Can total team buy-in be accomplished?

When recruiting, I sought candidates with a proven history of setting and achieving goals, and I considered a college degree a significant accomplishment regardless of the degree that was earned. Their employment history was critical. Was it suc-cessful? It was a red flag if someone changed jobs often. If employed, what would their current supervisor say about them? How creative were they when they were seeking an interview? How well did they prepare for the interview? How were they dressed? Generally, it's better to be a little overdressed than underdressed. Did they ask good questions? How often did they try to trial close during the interview, and did they ask for the job? Did they have a comprehensive and concise resume accompanied by a cover letter? Did it include a variety of highly qualified references? Did they have a documented list of interview questions?

Later in my sales leadership career I worked for a company that utilized personality assessment tests to objectively evaluate every new employee. I found them to be very accurate and an effective recruitment tool.

Don't be afraid to use your instincts. I made some of my best hires instinctively after one interview, based totally on the candidates' preparation, presentation, and answers to questions. If a candidate could adequately prepare and deliver a presentation to persuade me, it suggested how they would prepare and present to our customers.

You cannot lead if you are afraid to take risks.

You need the confidence and courage to make changes critical to the organization's success, which may sometimes involve unpopular decisions. You cannot lead if you are afraid to take risks. What do you do if one of your top producers causes team problems and cultural dysfunction? Is losing that top producer or the entire team a greater risk?

First, do your best to discover the cause of the dysfunction. This issue may be addressed by considering the employee's perspective or taking a deeper dive to understand what motivates the challenging employee. Top producers often have problems with teammates they perceive as not carrying their weight. Should you consider creating an exit strategy for the employee? The answer to that question could make or break your team culture. Remember, you are the leader and you are responsible.

Chris was a sales manager at one of our top competitors. He and his team were considered good competition, but his top seller consistently caused issues with the other team members. He regularly achieved his monthly revenue objectives and was responsible for as much as 30 percent of their total revenue. However, he seldom adhered to the company's policies and procedures. He was consistently late for work and rarely participated in meetings. His arrogance and total lack of empathy drove his administrative team to the point of resignation. Chris examined multiple approaches, including modifying established procedures and enlisting the support of a sales assistant to ensure the timely completion of all necessary documentation. He sought to understand the reason behind the employee's attitude that was damaging team culture.

Success is often dependent on doing things you don't like to do.

The solution was more straightforward than Chris realized. There will be occasions when it becomes necessary to risk short-term success for long-term gains. Success is often dependent on doing things you don't like to do. Deciding to terminate a team member's employment is sometimes necessary, though difficult, depending on the circumstances.

Sometimes the most talented people are the most challenging to lead.

Once you have the right people in the right seats, work to create a motivating environment where self-motivated individuals can maximize their talents and abilities. My initial one-on-one meetings with each team member were designed to understand their motivations and identify their short-term and long-term objectives.

Their shared information helped create a more effective compensation strategy that included special recognition opportunities.

Motivation vs. Inspiration

Be inspiring. Inspiration is internal, whereas motivation requires an external stimulus. It stems from a deep desire to achieve a goal, combined with your ability to connect emotionally. To inspire means to excite and encourage. Be an encourager. Talented people flourish when led by an inspiring and encouraging leader. The best leaders are those who build, nurture, support, and enhance.

I had an outstanding team, consisting of highly talented individuals. Once everyone's emotions had settled after the management change, it was time to lay out a vision that the team would follow and a leadership style that would produce the best results.

Review Questions

- What tools do you use to evaluate your team?
- What leaders have inspired you and how?
- What was an unpopular decision that you had to make? Share the story.
- How have you inspired the team?
- What have you used to motivate the team?

29

Vision, Mission, and Purpose

"People with vision see beyond belief, over the horizon."

—DeWayne Wickham, Dean Emeritus of Global Journalism & Communication, Morgan State University

WE HAD A good team, and the next step was to create a vision, mission, and purpose that the team would follow and support. I made it a point to include everyone in the process. Welcoming their opinions would be the first step in forming an inclusive culture. Our station was considered the underdog compared to our sister radio station, a well-branded station established in the 1920s. Customers assumed their sales team members were the best in the market because of the station's positive image, experience, and years of service.

What vision would illustrate the team's aspirations and goals? Our team and one-on-one meetings with the staff were valuable sources of information, and my prior involvement in the team culture as a team member before becoming the team sales manager was particularly beneficial. My positive relationship with most everyone on staff in every department was also a valuable benefit.

Effective leadership requires a thorough understanding of the DNA of each individual on staff and the chemistry of the team. Our team members were people who possessed strong personalities with a burning desire to win. They believed they were the best sales team with the best radio station in the market. Our station had the best ratings, great on-air talent, financial resources, and an excellent support team, which helped create a clear vision that the team could grasp and the market would respect.

A clear vision, supported by the team, enables leadership to make informed decisions that the team will follow. All our activities were aligned with our team's vision, mission, and purpose. When you have team buy-in, holding the team accountable is more seamless.

The vision, mission, and purpose describe where you are going, what you are doing, and why you do it. Each is an illustration of your company's personality. Your vision tells the story of what you strive to be. Where do you want your company to be in the consumer's mind 5, 10, or 100 years from now? Your vision should be challenging and perceived as unattainable by many. But as a team leader, you need to believe it can be done if you want your team to believe it can be done. Creating a vision is one of the most important tasks of leadership.

Including your team in the creation of a mission and mission statement is a good idea. This becomes an opportunity to give your team "skin in the game." Facilitate a brainstorming session. Welcome every idea, no matter how out-of-the-box. It's a great team-building opportunity as well.

Your purpose identifies your differentiator. It's the reason you are in business. Your purpose is simple—the reason why you open your doors every day. Everyone on the team should have a granular understanding of the company's reason for being in business, and senior leadership's actions must align with their stated goals.

I considered it crucial to involve the entire team in developing all three: vision, mission, and purpose. These goals were considered the North Star that would guide us when making decisions. Our future activities always focused on satisfying one or more of the three.

We branded our team "Team WAMZ."

Vision Statement:

Team WAMZ will strive to be the most respected broadcast sales team in the metropolitan area. We will endeavor to cultivate a positive culture that attracts the best talent and to be recognized as the best broadcast sales team in America.

Mission Statement:

Team WAMZ will work diligently to create innovative marketing solutions that deliver exceptional results. We will be empathetic to our customers' needs while providing service beyond expectations.

Purpose Statement:

Team WAMZ will exemplify authenticity and trustworthiness. We will utilize our platform to meet our customers' needs while achieving our station and individual goals and objectives.

The phrase "Team WAMZ" was painted on the wall of our sales arena. On the opposite wall, a framed poster read, "They don't care what you know until they know that you care." We tried to let our deeds speak louder than our words. The team became very successful, in large part because of its focus on the vision, mission, and purpose.

Review Questions

- Does your team have a clear vision?
- Do your actions reflect your purpose?
- Do your actions reflect your mission?
- How do you create team unity?
- How do you use your vision, mission, and purpose when interacting with customers?

30

Leadership Style

Leadership style creates team culture, good or bad.

BETH WAS THE general manager of a network television station and advanced through the ranks quickly due to her exceptional work ethic. She was a workaholic. She started each day at 6:00 a.m. and was seen many nights after 8:00 p.m. She was also detail-oriented and expected the same from all her direct reports. Beth had a dictating leadership style. She had absolute authority and didn't mind letting everyone know. It was very unrealistic for her team to work as many hours per week as she did. However, those who adhered to her demands received all the positive incentives. It was either her way or the doorway. She used punitive techniques to motivate her team rather than positive reinforcement for a job well done.

Beth's reputation grew within the industry, making recruitment and retaining top talent more challenging. She had little empathy for her team's family requirements. Her focus was work first, family second—and many times third. Excessive employee turnover and unrealistic expectations adversely affected all the metrics used to evaluate the station's performance. This was an example of the leadership myth recognized in a previous chapter. Great salespeople don't always make great sales leaders. It's challenging for some people to transition from "me" to "we."

There are several different leadership styles. Most have been and continue to be effective, depending on your situation. I quickly made it known that a traditional leadership style would not be part of my team's culture. I aimed to collaborate with each staff member to create a culture of honesty, trust, open communication, collective decision-making, and team focus. I made a point never to ask a team member to do a task I was unwilling to do myself. The team was very familiar with my personality, so it was essential to lead by example. People follow deeds quicker than promises.

I have always believed in the power of collaborative leadership. I sought collaboration when making individual or team decisions, resulting in productive outcomes throughout my leadership career. Its implementation was seamless because it mirrored my personality. A collaborative leader encourages teamwork and collaboration among all team members, regardless of role or title. It helped create and promote an open-door culture that welcomed new ideas. This was very different from a traditional top-down management approach. It was more of a participative, open, and horizontal approach. My staff was opinionated, positive, and open to every idea. Problem-solving was a team effort whenever possible, and the results were incredible. We were a team and sought every reason to celebrate individual and team accomplishments.

People follow deeds quicker than promises.

I understood the importance of consistent decision-making. When you have a consistent problem-solving style, your staff will know how you'll answer questions before they are asked. I asked every team member to accompany problems with a possible solution. Many problems were solved with little input from me, and it also helped prove that I valued their opinion.

It was essential to convey expectations verbally and in writing to ensure mutual agreement and promote cultural accountability. Each staff member had to adhere to established policies and procedures, yet I understood that different personalities required a different leadership approach. People are motivated for various reasons, but I never focused on what divided my team; instead, our shared values, interests, and purpose were the center of attention.

We had a diverse and talented sales team with various styles and backgrounds, with shared motivations, values, and interests. One member of our team was a good leader and aspired to get a management position. It was very important to him, so I put him in a leadership position as often as possible. He was a good thinker and had been in the business for several years. He was a very influential team member, and I valued his opinion. I wanted him to know how much he was appreciated without alienating the other staff members. He was highly respected in the broadcast sales industry and was an outstanding relationship developer.

Another team member demonstrated strong creativity and a focus on family values. She was passionate—the glue that helped keep the team happy and promoted teamwork. She led almost every special event. I always tried to find the resources for her ideas and promotions. On one occasion, we provided elephant rides for one of her customers. It was a win-win promotion. Our customers and our listeners loved it. She presented several out-of-the-box ideas, and I did my best to support as many as possible.

The senior member of the team provided the best customer service. She would help her clients move furniture, cut the grass, and other things most salespeople would consider outside their job description. She was also a creative and outstanding artist with a very eccentric imagination. I didn't appreciate her as much as I should have until she retired. She had an extensive account list, and we lost about 30 percent of her billing revenue after her retirement. Many of her customers continued to include our radio station, but we lost share when she retired. Her customers included the station because they loved her, as well as the results the radio station could deliver. Her relationships became friendships. It was also an example of how turnover, for whatever reason, can negatively affect your results. It was a valuable lesson: Maximize strengths and manage weaknesses.

Four other team members brought their unique talents and proved to be good salespeople. We only lost one person during my transition to sales manager.

I rarely harbored animosity toward any team member who believed another employment opportunity would better meet their professional or personal needs. I would often help if they asked. Toward the end of my media sales leadership career, I began to recognize that the chances of retaining millennials and Gen Z salespeople on staff for over three years were slim. Money was not as significant an issue as I had previously believed. It was a prime example of the necessity to stay aware of market trends and remain open to change.

We had a good team, and we all worked together to make it a great team; each member had their niche. I welcomed every opportunity to help them "soar with their strengths"—to find their sales sweet spot. We were Team WAMZ, proud of our accomplishments and highly confident. Everyone on the team recognized that their actions or inactions could impact the entire group.

Review Questions

- What leadership style do you believe is the most effective?
- Are your team members included in problem-solving? If so, how?
- When have you experienced outstanding leadership, and why?
- When have you experienced poor leadership, and why?
- Have you ever resigned from a company because of a poor leader?

31

Team Building

Team success requires successful team building.

OUR CORE MEMBERS were established, and my leadership style positioned them to meet and exceed their team and individual goals and objectives. All members fully embraced the team's vision, mission, and purpose. It was the ideal time to add new talent to the sales team. The station's success generated considerable buzz in the market—several experienced sales professionals from other radio stations considered joining the team.

Recruitment is a continuous process.

A leader's ability to evaluate and attract talent will significantly influence their success or failure. Recruiting and retaining talent is vital to a leader's strategic plan. Recruitment is a continuous process. One of my mentors shared the importance of "Always be recruiting." Having a solid talent funnel is a good strategy to help minimize the pain of losing a team member, and it doesn't hurt for the team to recognize that you are always looking for new talent.

Candidate Categories

There are primarily two categories of employee candidates. The first is the unemployed candidate. On most occasions, these candidates must secure employment within a specified timeline. They are recent college graduates, ex-military personnel, or those who might have been terminated, been downsized, or have resigned from a recent employer. The latter two are reasons they might or might not honestly share with a new potential employer.

The second is the employed candidate. Understanding the reasons behind an individual's decision to leave their current employer is important. It helps you to understand their motivations. Are they seeking increased compensation, advancement opportunities, a better work environment, more flexibility, a better culture, or a career that better aligns with their passions?

I successfully hired candidates from both categories and found that obtaining information about employed candidates was more seamless. For instance, if they were successful sales professionals representing competing radio stations or another marketing platform, it was feasible to obtain the necessary information from a current team member or a shared customer.

Resumes only give you a reason to interview and are seldom the only reason to hire.

Make it a goal to hire people who are currently or potentially better than you. This starts with an honest self-assessment of your strengths and weaknesses. Hire the best, clearly communicate expectations, and empower them to perform their jobs effectively. Realize it's not possible to be great at everything. I have worked for managers who had to be involved with every aspect of the business, and it was an unpleasant experience.

They had a problem with trusting their staff. Trust and lack of trust are also among what author Patrick Lencioni labels *The Five Dysfunctions of a Team*—also the title of his book.

Be deliberate. You will need to live with the people you hire. If you have been in leadership for an extended period and are responsible for hiring, there are probably occasions when you have made a bad hire. A hire can be described as bad for a variety of reasons: They exaggerate their competence; they struggle to perform in the culture; they lack confidence or courage; or they are influenced by outside factors that hinder their progress, among other issues. Interviewers will do their best to embellish their strengths and disguise their weaknesses. I sought to hire high-character people, recognizing that poor hiring decisions would cost me time and money. Throughout my 29-year sales leadership career, I have had the opportunity to hire very competent people who lacked confidence, those who were confident but misrepresented their competence, and those who lacked the courage to ask difficult questions.

Develop a standard onboarding process. You want every new employee to have a great start, regardless of position. It benefits the leader, the organization, and the new hire. Sales careers can be gratifying when accompanied by a clear plan, strategy, system, and process.

Onboarding Process

It starts with a welcoming approach. Congratulate your new hire publicly and in writing for accepting your career opportunity. I mentioned earlier that making a positive or negative first impression only takes three to six seconds. Ensure their work area is clean and that all necessary tools for performing their duties are ready, available, up-to-date, and operational.

You should also provide a facility tour and introductions to current employees. It can be challenging when a new employee is unfamiliar with the building, and the current staff do not recognize the new person.

It is important to be honest with your new hire. Let them know about your training process and who is involved in helping to prepare them to succeed. Share the good, the bad, and the ugly. Revisit your leadership style. Communicate expectations meticulously and secure mutual agreement. Verbal agreements have little value if not documented and signed off on. Schedule one-on-ones daily for the first few weeks and possibly more, depending on their level of competence. The time you spend with a new hire early in the process will help you recognize quickly if you've made a great, good, or bad hire.

Let them know they will be held accountable. But accountability goes both ways. Do not be afraid to be held accountable yourself. Avoidance of accountability is another of Patrick Lencioni's five dysfunctions of a team.

Occasionally, consider allowing a few current team members to meet your top candidates before hiring. They often can provide a different but valuable perspective.

Communicating your leadership style and accurately describing your culture can prevent you from making a bad hire.

The style that has worked for you and your team should not be adjusted for one person.

Some people thrive in a structured work environment, while others perceive it as micromanagement. Transparency about management style will help both you and the candidate before you add them to the team.

Review Questions

- What are a few of your team-building techniques?
- Have you succeeded more with employed or unemployed new-hire candidates, and why?
- What is your usual hiring process?
- Have you ever made a bad hire? If so, what were the reasons?
- What are a few features of your onboarding process?

32

Team Culture

Your ability to create a great team culture is your best defense against team member turnover. People don't leave companies; they leave people.

THE TEAM AND I had created an inclusive, respectful, fun, and productive culture. Our culture had inspired our talented team to reach its full potential. It was a culture rooted in trust, accountability, teamwork, and goal achievement. Most team members consistently achieved their financial goals. Their hard work increased the demand on our inventory, which created the need for new sales professionals. It was essential to recruit salespeople who would align with our current team's vision, mission, and purpose, while possessing the characteristics exemplified by the four Cs: competence, confidence, courage, and character. They had to be entrepreneurial and have the ability to hit the ground running after their 30-day training process. We had built a team that was the envy of the market.

There were challenges. Problems and challenges are a part of doing business, but the team had become so incredibly cohesive that every problem seemed manageable. There was a high level of trust and belief; everyone did their part to help achieve team and individual sales success. It was a unique group. They were competitive, yet friendly and respectful. I welcomed their children into the office when there were child-care issues, and on Take Your Child to Work days. Sometimes they brought their dogs if they were well-trained. Family always came first. Whenever a staff member's family was in need, we were there to help. The team attended funerals, weddings, and other special events.

I believed in the saying "Being nice is more important than being important." It doesn't require any extra effort to be kind to others. Kindness doesn't represent weakness; it represents strength. You can be kind while holding your team account-able. The few times when my kindness was misunderstood, it was clarified quickly. If the misunderstanding continued, I had the courage to make a team change. As they say, "If you can't change the people around you, change the people around you." I tried to demonstrate thoughtfulness consistently and led with kindness throughout my career. Leading with kindness can help create a great culture, but it's only effective if you have the right people in the right seats on the team. It's hard if you're not led with kindness.

Our station culture helped make our sales employment oppor-tunities the most sought-after in the area. With the help of senior leadership, I established an incentive program that included weekend trips to the Bahamas, team outings on the lake, and special recognitions from the CEO, as well as oppor-tunities to earn more money that the entire team would share. The sales team was allowed to support nonprofit organizations and host customer appreciation events that were the envy of the market. Their success was shared with every station employee, including on-air staff, sales assistants, production, news, and traffic teams. Our sales team expanded from 7 rep-resentatives to 13, and our gross revenue increased from $3 million to $11 million over the next 10 years. The team's yearly revenue objectives were achieved in 9 of those 10 years.

Friendliness vs. Friendships

Your motivation to be friendly can affect your team's culture. However, a significant distinction exists between being friendly and being a friend. Maintaining a level of distance between you and the people you supervise is wise. Use discretion when interacting in a social environment. Be mindful of your alcohol consumption, if you drink at all. If your team is at an event with alcohol, monitor the drinking and ensure everyone gets home safely. Friendliness can sometimes be misunderstood. You should never be surprised by what people will do to survive difficult situations. There have been occasions when I have been disappointed by the people I nurtured the most.

Be sure to compose text messages and emails with care and attention to detail. Once you hit send, they are in the receiver's possession forever. Developing authentic staff friendships is possible, but rare.

When transitioning from team member to team leader, your interaction style must also change. Occasionally, a team member who views you as a friend may anticipate special treatment and feel disappointed due to your commitment to consistent decision-making, particularly when those decisions impact the entire team. Have an open and candid conversation to explain your motivation and ensure fairness to everyone on the team.

I experienced incredible success by leading with a kind spirit and adhering to The Golden Rule: "Treat people like you want to be treated." You can be friendly and treat your staff with kindness while still holding them accountable. You will find that most people have no problem being held accountable when you have a collaborative leadership style. The benefits of creating a kind, friendly, and nurturing culture has the potential to exceed your expectations. But never forget, they work for you.

Review Questions

- How would you describe your work environment culture?
- How does your staff contribute to a positive culture?
- What actions can you take to help create a positive culture?
- Who are your culture champions?
- Who are your culture busters?

33

Responsibility

Be inspired to give your team ownership for success and be motivated to take personal ownership for team failures.

I HAD A team member exclude important information in a written presentation to one of our high-revenue-generating customers. The mistake had the potential to cost the station thousands of dollars and tarnish an excellent relationship. When the error was discovered, I took the initiative to call the customer and proactively take total responsibility. She seemed surprised that I made the call rather than the employee who created the proposal, but she appreciated my approach, and we worked together to create a solution.

On another occasion, our top revenue-generating account underwent a leadership change, and their new advertising agency president requested that I remove the current account salesperson due to a communication issue. The salesperson was an excellent sales professional who had provided outstanding service for over 10 years; additionally, the account represented 20 percent of her monthly revenue. I risked losing the account, but asked the agency president to give her three months to prove her value. He agreed, and she remained the account representative until her retirement more than 10 years later. It demonstrated to the entire staff that I was willing to risk one of the station's most valuable accounts to support a teammate, particularly if it was an honest mistake.

Taking responsibility leads to earning the trust and respect of your team. When a leader assumes responsibility for the actions of their team, it demonstrates a high level of competence, confidence, courage, and character. Strong leaders communicate both good news and bad news effectively. I tried to support every team member, regardless of their achievements or mistakes. Punitive methods were seldom, if ever, used when dealing with errors. They were used as coaching opportunities. My rule was to avoid making the same error more than once. My policy was to honor every proposal presented to a customer, regardless of the circumstances. Responsibility means keeping your word. I believed the company logo was a representation of that word.

If you mess up, fess up, and most people will help rescue you if you give them an opportunity. An identified, understood, and attacked problem is a practically solved problem.

Be honest, take responsibility, but never make the same mistake twice.

Don't accept leadership opportunities if you are not willing to take responsibility.

Great leaders accept responsibility.

Review Questions

- Can you share an example of a time you took responsibility?
- What is your method of handling mistakes?
- How do you honor commitments?
- What does responsibility mean to you?
- Do you lead by example? If so, describe three instances.

34

Coaching

Success requires talent and great coaching, but a great-coached team can defeat a more talented team.

THROUGHOUT MY ENTIRE leadership career, I have led with my heart while focusing on exceeding goals and objectives. I also understood the importance of maximizing the potential of every staff member. A good coach has the same characteristics as a good teacher. An important part of effective coaching is your ability to nurture. An empathetic approach to coaching will not only help improve your team's competence, it will also help support a trusting culture. Coaching is a crucial component of sales leadership. An enthusiastic approach to coaching helps build positive relationships.

I frequently used one of my football coaches as a barometer for outstanding coaching. Coach Morrison was a great person and an exceptional coach. He had the unique ability to push the team harder than almost every other coach on staff, but he was also the most caring of them all. He knew how to get the most out of his players, but possessed a nurturing spirit. He helped each team member recognize and realize their full potential. Coach Morrison was always willing to help anyone at any time. He understood that there were times when family issues had to be satisfied. However, he would hold you accountable in the classroom and on the football field. He taught life skills with the same enthusiasm as teaching techniques on how to protect your quarterback.

All great coaches possess the same characteristics and the courage to give honest assessments. Coaching is your opportunity to shape the destiny of your team members. Once the right people are in the right seats, it's a leader's responsibility to help each person reach their full potential. Like a good teacher, good coaches know how to assess the needs of each individual on a team. There is a difference between being the best and being the best you can be. Good coaches never stop coaching. It is an ongoing journey. They work to help you find your sweet spot no matter what career you choose to pursue.

Occasionally a member of your staff might think they know it all and be unwilling to learn new techniques or improve their existing skills. This person is likely to harm your culture, so it might be time for them to find a new opportunity.

The best coaches are selfless. They remove their egos from the process as much as possible. They become good coaches because they are personally invested in the improvement of each team member.

Good coaches are active listeners. They listen without judgment as much as possible. Listening is another opportunity to exhibit empathy. Focused listening means giving a person your undivided attention.

It's challenging, but the best communicators are focused and engaged listeners. Take notes whenever possible. It will help you remember how you wanted to respond.

The phrase "They don't care what you know until they know that you care" was mentioned in a previous chapter. It was printed, framed, and placed on the wall in our sales arena. I took every opportunity to show my team members that I cared in every way possible. I listened to their problems and challenges, prioritizing God and family first. My sales teams worked hard for me. I made an effort to be consistent in my decision-making. What I did for one, I tried to do for all.

One-on-One Meetings

One-on-one meetings with each staff member provide individual coaching opportunities.

This is their time to share their concerns, challenges, and victories. I ensured that each staff member received a minimum of an hour of undivided attention. You should limit interruptions, avoid early evaluations, and ask open-ended questions to get a better understanding of each salesperson's needs and challenges. I also used silence as one of my most effective communication tools. I made a point never to interrupt anyone before they finished talking. It's important to set clear expectations. The success of one-on-ones depends on thorough preparation. Our meeting preparation included sharing the following:

- A list of weekly scheduled appointments
- Copies of sales proposals
- Weekly, monthly, and quarterly business projections/ forecasts
- A list of target customers to help with any needed step in the sales process
- Occasional one-on-one ride-alongs—scheduled or unscheduled

The meetings were designed to be a safe place. Participants were allowed to share every situation, whether business or personal.

They were also opportunities to practice and create role-playing sessions. The team found these to be challenging, but necessary. Improvement requires practice to help overcome weaknesses and enhance strengths. Some people loved to role-play, but most didn't. One-on-one meetings provided an opportunity to establish trust and rapport. Make improving one step of the sales process a part of your weekly one-on-ones and your sales meetings. Enhancing your sales fundamentals should always be a consistent focus.

My sales teams enjoyed their one-on-one meetings. They were cheerful and upbeat. They knew what was said in those meetings would not be shared if they asked it not to be shared. A member of one of my sales teams asked why I believed we needed to meet every week. She felt that twice a month would be more appropriate. I strongly disagreed, and soon my meetings with her were incredibly productive. Three months later, I could not keep her out of my office. The times when business was good were the times to make it better. I often told my team, "The only way to coast is downhill. Take advantage of good times because good times don't last forever." During challenging times, I utilized one-on-one meetings to encourage and help generate ideas. Good times are not the time to get overconfident, and bad times are not the time to give up.

Sales Meetings

Sales meetings were used to train, share ideas, and build team unity and trust. It was a time to hold teammates accountable without making it personal. They won together and lost together. The key was staying together. It was their opportunity to talk and listen. Communication will always be an ongoing challenge. Good communication is a journey. Great teams create an environment of accountability, especially during sales meetings. I worked to eliminate the "fear of conflict," which is also one of the five dysfunctions characterized in Patrick Lencioni's book *The Five Dysfunctions of a Team*. Most everyone was allowed to share their issues if they were delivered respectfully.

Sales meetings should have a clear agenda and be well-prepared in advance. We focused on many of the same issues and challenges discussed in our one-on-one meetings: problem accounts, overcoming objections, monthly and quarterly forecasts, accounts receivable, and victories to celebrate. I made it mandatory for sales team members to lead one sales meeting at least three times per year. The person leading the meeting was tasked with creating the agenda. The results were amazing. Our meetings lasted about an hour. I seldom allowed them to become gripe sessions, and when they were allowed, they didn't last very long. We worked to make them positive and inspirational. Our office was a safe place, especially during our meetings.

If you want to demotivate your sales team, consider cutting their commissions due to their success.

I was never bothered by how much money they made, and I helped them maximize their earnings. I never understood why some companies would adjust their salesperson compensation plans based on sales success. Sales leaders are also responsible for managing sales costs. However, when our sales team exceeded expectations, I acknowledged and celebrated their financial accomplishments.

If you want to demotivate your sales team, consider cutting their commissions due to their success.

An effective coach will enhance at least one step of the sales process and diligently work to mitigate threats and eliminate obstacles daily.

Review Questions

- What are the characteristics of an effective coach?
- Who were some of your better coaches, and why?
- What is your definition of a nurturing environment?
- How are your one-on-ones structured?
- How are your sales meetings structured?

35

Attitude

Attitudes, whether positive or negative, are contagious.

SHARON WAS A sales professional for a competing radio station. She had an excellent reputation for being a straight shooter, and was formidable competition on the streets. She seemed to be everywhere, regularly offering customers a competitive alternative at a significantly lower cost. She was doing well until her sales manager got reassigned to another market. Her new sales manager turned her world upside down. Their personalities clashed from the moment they met. Sharon's previous manager was people-oriented, trusted her team, and had a nurturing disposition. Her new sales manager was just the opposite. Her untrusting attitude created a demotivating culture and poor team morale. The team's attitude began to mirror that of their new manager, and it was reflected in their poor performance. Sharon's new manager was an example of a bad boss.

A bad boss may not be a bad person. Often it's a bad fit. A bad boss can be a good person, but may feel the need to constantly remind you that they are the boss. They may believe that leadership requires constant control, overlooking the value of empathy, kindness, and collaboration. A bad boss may be someone who embellishes weaknesses and minimizes strengths. They are entirely task-oriented; it's either "their way or the highway." They want tasks completed with little concern for those performing the task or interest in ideas contrary to theirs. They are inflexible and prioritize system adherence over achieving goals and objectives. They surround themselves with yes people and fail to value diversity. Many are insecure and afraid that there are people on their staff who may be better than themselves. Few workplace situations are worse than working for a bad boss. People don't resign from companies; they resign from people.

Your attitude will help or hurt your team through good and challenging times. Good leaders know how to inspire through difficult times. It all starts with a positive attitude. There will be occasions when nothing seems to be working. It seems that the harder you work, the more difficult it becomes. Your attitude will get you through a storm. The positive message that you tell yourself will help you deliver a positive message to your team. Do not project doubt! Storms come, and storms end, and spring always follows winter.

Successful leaders understand the importance of always projecting a positive image. They have the unique ability to see the glass half full rather than half empty. A leader's positive attitude and enthusiasm can create an enthusiastic team. They always try to look for the best in people, whether it be staff, friends, or people they meet for the first time. A friendly and kind attitude can be both motivating and inspiring. A leader's attitude can help their staff achieve results beyond what they believed was possible. It enables them to think outside their comfort zone. Comfort is one of the greatest enemies of success. Help your team mentally visualize the rewards that can be achieved through their positive thinking and positive attitude.

Most people's attitudes, positive or negative, are created by life's experiences. People are not born with a positive or negative attitude any more than they are born good or bad leaders. Some view problems as opportunities, and others see them as insurmountable. They are the first to give up. They don't understand that problems help create innovation. This is one of the many reasons staffing is the most crucial task for a leader.

One of the greatest enemies of progress is comfort. As previously stated, never coast. Change is inevitable. It is your choice to either be a facilitator or a change recipient. Either way, your situation will change. It is up to you to either be proactive or reactive. If you experience softer-than-expected market conditions, resulting in many customers either reducing or canceling their advertising campaigns, it may be time to shift your team's positive attitude into positive action and explore unconventional revenue-generating opportunities. Good teams became stronger through adversity, and leaders became more effective.

Leaders must maintain a positive attitude, regardless of the situation's difficulty. As author John C. Maxwell said, "Leadership is influence." Your team is watching your every step. This is the time to show leadership by how you handle adversity. These are the occasions when you earn the respect of your team. Run through challenging situations, and you will emerge a better and stronger leader. Try your best to surround yourself with people who exhibit a winning attitude. Avoid doubters/haters. If you believe you will, you certainly will; if you don't, you certainly will not.

Don't overthink it. Don't get caught up in a thought storm that causes decision-making doubt. Decide and move on. Critical thinking can be the catalyst that transforms doubt into a positive attitude, and a positive attitude can, in turn, become the catalyst for critical thinking. They are not mutually exclusive.

Review Questions

- What strategies do you use to navigate through challenging times?
- How has your attitude affected your desired results?
- Do you see the value of leading with kindness? If so, share how.
- How do your deeds reflect your attitude?
- How do you use critical thinking to support your attitude?

36

Beliefs and Willpower

*Overwhelming challenges are necessary to create
incredible accomplishments.*

JORDYN POSSESSED QUALITIES that could positively contribute to
any team, regardless of their goals and objectives. She always
explored the positive in every situation and never seemed to
have a bad day. She was the team cheerleader. She bought
birthday cakes for the support staff, cookies for holidays, and
donuts on at least one Friday per month. She possessed a
self-determination that transcended the beliefs of most of the
staff. She believed in her ability to exceed all expectations.
If a radio station group was at more than 90 percent of their
monthly revenue goal with less than two weeks to go, most
people would believe achieving their revenue objectives was
very unlikely. Not Jordyn. If they were at 80 percent or better,
she would rally the team, often without her sales manager, and
they would devise a strategy to get it done. Her belief in the
team was so overwhelming that it forced everyone to participate. Their manager had to negotiate with the programming
team for additional commercial inventory.

There is power in believing all your goals will be achieved.
I had to believe that I would become a sales manager long

before the opportunity presented itself. I had a mental image of myself sitting in my manager's chair, and I started to act the part. Whenever they hired a new salesperson, I would take the leadership role of the new employee trainer. Senior management didn't ask; I volunteered.

Successful leaders instill a sense of belief in every person on the team. Every team member has to believe that they will reach and exceed their goals and objectives. The feeling of belief is inspiring: It seeds action, and action seeds accomplishments. The sales team believed they could achieve their goals, and they consistently delivered extraordinary work when the goals seemed unachievable. Jordyn always led the way. Their belief and willpower helped fuel other positive characteristics, such as persistence, perseverance, and critical thinking. They conducted a brainstorming session where all ideas that did not compromise their policies and procedures were considered. All five of the Sales Success Principles also apply to sales leadership.

Overwhelming desire and unwavering belief ignite persistence. Every great accomplishment was achieved because a person believed it could be achieved.

Keep your goals and aspirations close to the vest. Don't share your thoughts with everybody. There is a reason that so few people reach their potential. Small minds often reject great ideas. Successful leaders infuse their team with a belief that the vision and mission can be accomplished.

Tom Brady, the greatest quarterback in NFL history, believed he could snatch victory from defeat, as did his teammates, fans, and often the opposing team. Regardless of the circumstances, no deficit was considered insurmountable.

Belief is an incredible mindset. Sometimes it's hard to explain, but belief is that powerful. Successful outcomes will help create future successful outcomes.

During the 2024 Olympic gold medal game against the French National team, Stephen Curry was another example of how a person's belief can influence the beliefs of his teammates and fans. The last shot he made over two defenders, after making three other three-point shots with seconds to play, was one of the most incredible shots at a significant moment ever witnessed. He was the only person alive who would have taken that shot during that situation—because he believed he could make it, and so did everyone else. If you can inspire your team to believe, your accomplishments will exceed your imagination.

Review Questions

- Who is your belief champion on your team, and why?
- What examples show how your belief helped you exceed expectations?
- How has your willpower helped you persevere? Give examples.
- When has your belief and willpower fueled critical and creative thinking?
- Can you share an example of how an overwhelming challenge created an incredible achievement?

37

Communication

One of the most significant problems with effective communication is not realizing you are the problem.

LACK OF COMMUNICATION and the presence of territorialism are significant barriers to reaching your sales sweet spot. I have discovered that effective communication is a two-way street. There have been instances where I presumed my message was being received, only to discover later that it was not. You should utilize every available tool. Different people learn differently. Some individuals are auditory learners, while others are visual learners, and still others perform better when information is communicated in writing. Use all three whenever possible. Send information and make verification an expectation. Effective communication is a journey. You are only as good as your last misinterpreted email or text message.

Territorialism can also be detrimental to team culture. I have seen people refuse to accept help from someone in a different department, knowing that success requires a team effort. A great team understands the importance of every person and every department within the organization. The team or department cannot claim success if the company as a whole is not successful. Achieving the company's vision, mission, and purpose should always be the focus. Territorialism will slow or stop innovation and new ideas. Leaders who are inspired to create a great culture love "what if" people. These are people who continually explore new ideas, no matter their primary responsibility.

Incorporate department cross-training. It's a good idea for every staff member to understand the responsibilities of people from every department. Make the process an expectation. Facilitating off-premises retreats as part of your team development strategy can also help lower the mental barriers that sometimes exist among different departments. Both ideas will help create team culture empathy.

When my sales teams celebrated success, we included everyone in every department. Consider setting up compensation based on the company reaching its goals—from the CEO to the environmental services staff.

Reaching your sales sweet spot depends on effective communication. It's the oil that primes the machine. I have never experienced a group or company that overcommunicates. Learn the importance of being an active listener. Reward the behavior you want to be repeated. Listening is a learned skill and is far more critical than speaking skills. I have found that one of the most effective ways to establish a positive relationship is by being open to listening to another person's opinion. The best mates, parents, friends, employees, or supervisors are the ones who understand and value the power of listening. One of the primary reasons for workplace conflict is a lack of, or perceived lack of, effective communication. Good communication must be intentional. There are several communication tools, yet it is still challenging to accomplish.

Learn to be concise, comprehensive, and engaging. Being thick-skinned and well-prepared is valuable. In a previous chapter, we discussed the importance of maintaining a positive attitude. Communication is more seamless when the giver and the receiver have an attitude that promotes active listening.

Review Questions

- Can you share an example of a conflict caused by poor communication?
- When did effective communication help solve a problem? Share details.
- What have you done to reduce territorialism?
- How has territorialism affected productivity?
- What strategy have you used to improve your active listening skills?

Part Three

Your character and your personality are not mutually exclusive.

The following four chapters focus on personality characteristics that often help distinguish between average, good, and great sales leaders. An entire chapter is devoted to understanding your personality and developing the intuition to understand the personalities of your customers and staff. However, your ability to build trust, your willingness to be authentic, your commitment to integrity, and your dedication to humility are all qualities of great leaders, and strengthen the other characteristics highlighted in previous chapters. Your ability to find your sweet spot as a sales leader increases when you have an open mind, a positive personality, a collaborative style, and an insatiable desire to improve.

38

Building Trust

Trust is the most valuable gift given and received.

A WORK ENVIRONMENT based on trust will help create an inviting culture. Regardless of your current situation, being considered trustworthy is extraordinarily valuable. Trust is the result of cultivating relationships that are important to you. It takes years to build, yet it can be destroyed in a moment. A staff member who trusts you will be willing to work hard for you. If you have hired the right people, they will want you to succeed in direct proportion to how much you demonstrate your desire to help them succeed.

The foundation of every great team is trust. There are varying levels of trust, depending on the nature of the relationship. I earned the trust of my sales team as a sales team member. However, gaining trust as their sales manager was a different level of trust altogether. I worked with them for over five years, and my results as a sales staff member were well documented. But how could my salesperson's acumen help to create team trust?

Trust is not a given; it's earned. And if you are going to gain someone's trust, they need to see how your leadership style will benefit each person on the team. Trust is built by helping others and keeping your promises. Trust is always accompanied by responsibility. It is essential for each person on a team to earn the trust of their colleagues. A leader must trust that each team member will work diligently to achieve both the team's objectives and their individual goals.

You establish trust when you do what you say you will do. Don't put yourself in a corner. Under-promise whenever possible. You can create expectations that deliver win-win outcomes. Here is an example: Don't promise you can complete a task on Wednesday when Friday is acceptable. If you complete the task on Thursday, you will have exceeded expectations. However, if you promise completion on Wednesday and are confronted with an unexpected issue beyond your control, resulting in the task being completed on Thursday, you are not meeting expectations. You will get the reputation of almost everyone else: "No one does what they say they are going to do, when they say they are going to do it."

....

Trust is built by helping others and keeping your promises.

....

This is another opportunity to consider the power of one more. Whatever the task, develop the discipline to do one more. Consistently doing one more than what you promised will not only help yield amazing results, but also help build a relationship based on trust. This was mentioned in a previous chapter. Displaying an empathic approach to solving your customers' challenges can also help build trust. When you can be relied on, and you selflessly display high character, you will build trust. Once you've earned trust, please do everything you can to not break it.

A St. Stephen Baptist Church senior staff member once said, "Breaking trust is like breaking a mug. You can glue it back together, but there will always be cracks." A team that does not trust its leader will never reach its full potential.

Leaders must also trust themselves. You will be required to make decisions that will affect the direction of your team, and often the short- and long-term success of your company. Consider all your options, make a decision, and trust that your training, experience, and instinct will deliver your desired results.

Review Questions

- How difficult is it for you to earn trust, and why?
- Are you trustworthy? If so, how?
- Do you complete tasks before they are promised?
- Do you keep promises no matter what?
- Has someone ever betrayed your trust? If so, how did you respond?

39

Authenticity

Your true value is being who you truly are.

I EARNED AN excellent reputation, and several broadcast companies sought my expertise as a sales leader. I considered it a compliment when recruiters presented new leadership opportunities. My transparent and friendly approach to sales and sales leadership helped me become a popular sales leader. I took pride in my ability to recruit, lead, and coach talented sales professionals. However, one of my leadership objectives was to "keep it real" as much as possible. You never had to guess what I was thinking; expectations were meticulously communicated, and agreement was always required. A collaborative and transparent leadership style will help increase employee retention. It's another opportunity to treat your staff the way you want to be treated. Not everyone will agree with your decisions, but they will appreciate your honesty. It's uncertainty that makes people uncomfortable.

You cannot be what you are not. Being authentic means recognizing who you are and openly embracing your beliefs and values. It is necessary to be honest with yourself and your team. You will lose your effectiveness as a leader and a coach if the team believes you are dishonest. You and your team are in the game together. Offensive linemen will fight to protect their quarterback because they have a shared vision, mission, and purpose. A good quarterback acknowledges excellent offensive line play because their success is interdependent. He must show respect for his linemen on and off the field. Remember, your team is watching your every move.

Everyone on the sales team knew the authentic me. I understood my strengths and weaknesses; they were always on full display. I had a very candid and open communication style, and never knowingly told them anything I knew was untrue. They all knew I would "keep it real," whether the news was good or bad. It has always been my goal to address problems and issues quickly. Being a consistent decision-maker can be challenging, but it helps create team harmony and a positive culture. They began to know how I would answer questions or address a problem before they asked. Most of my sales teams experienced exceptional success. If they fell short of their revenue goals, we explored every opportunity to achieve the next objective.

I mentioned before that it was important for all our team members to try to create a solution for every problem before asking for my help. It worked like a charm. It proved that I valued their opinion and often used their solutions. It allowed every team member to have "some skin in the game" and be partly responsible for successful results. There were a few instances when sensitive information could not be shared. However, I shared as much as possible with the team as often as possible. The best way to manage your weaknesses is to recognize them and develop a solution strategy. Most members of every sales team I led felt comfortable sharing business and personal problems.

I had a salesperson who was reluctant to invest in our 401(k) that offered a 5 percent match. She started to invest because of my counsel, and 10 years later she thanked me for putting her in a position to retire.

There was a salesperson on my team who was reluctant to call on a customer due to the customer's reputation for being a tough negotiator. I forced her to call because I knew she had the courage and just needed encouragement. I told her that I believed in her and that she could accomplish it. She and the customer developed a very fruitful relationship, and she earned more money that year than at any other time in her career.

Another senior sales team member was uncomfortable when I asked him to allow me to help with a few of his key accounts. He eventually realized that my influence would help him achieve his revenue objectives. The strategy was very successful, and we called at least one of his key accounts during most of our weekly one-on-one meetings.

There was another salesperson who had a combination of high academic intelligence, street smarts, and a heavy dose of common sense. He was a single father with two young sons, and he and I often discussed fatherhood and its importance. I was always there to give advice. Recently, one son graduated with an engineering degree, and the other finished his senior year as a member of a college football team.

I had an authentic passion for helping people be their best, whether in business or personal matters. Those are just a few success stories among the hundreds I've experienced during my leadership career. We established a culture where being authentic was the norm and not the exception.

Review Questions

- How much do you value authenticity?
- How has recognizing your strengths and weaknesses been a benefit?
- How do you let your staff know the real you?
- How comfortable are you when a teammate asks for personal advice?
- How do you use being real to solve problems and issues?

40

Integrity

Integrity is telling the truth, no matter the consequences.

DEVYN'S SALES MANAGER often tasked her with recruiting new sales team prospects. He asked Devyn if she would help recruit Sharon, who was mentioned in a previous chapter. She was the salesperson who was assigned a new sales manager with an authoritative leadership style. Everyone knew she would welcome a new opportunity, but three other companies vied to add her to their sales team. Devyn had a way about herself that was not easy to describe. She had a high degree of integrity, was very trustworthy, and uncompromising. If there was a person who was honest to a fault, it would be Devyn. She had an infectious personality and quickly developed relationships.

Sharon and Devyn bonded quickly, and Devyn's manager's impeccable reputation made adding Sharon to their team seamless. Sharon was aware of Devyn's reputation and was excited to be a member of the team. Devyn's customers loved her, and Sharon was happy that they would be teammates and not competitors.

The team had a culture founded in trust and integrity—two of the most significant virtues any salesperson or sales leader can possess. Trust and integrity are not mandatory for leadership; they are mandatory for outstanding leadership. Trust and integrity work well in tandem. A person with a low degree of integrity cannot be trusted. Devyn and Sharon's sales manager was considered an honest and reliable individual. He took pride in being considered a person of high integrity and felt it was his greatest compliment. Your level of integrity will mirror your beliefs and values. It reflects your relationship with your family, your charitable motivation, and your empathy for the needs of others.

I supported my team when senior leadership proposed policy changes that my staff considered unfavorable. I tried to understand my team's concerns when I believed the decision would hurt the individual or the station's progress. On one occasion, senior leadership sought to reduce a salesperson's commission rate due to their overwhelming success. They made more money than expected, but the company exceeded its projected profits by over 40 percent. I had to persuade senior leadership that the change would hinder growth, negatively impact morale, and affect the returns for next year. They agreed not to make the changes, but said they would reevaluate their decision at the end of the following year.

My collaborative and people-oriented leadership style consistently produced outstanding results. There are numerous examples of my team members giving an extra effort to help me, as well as themselves. They wanted me to succeed as much as I wanted each of them to succeed. There was a salesperson on one of my teams who made an honest mistake during an event promotion. It was suggested that we not pay the commission the salesperson earned for selling and servicing the event. It was a terrible suggestion. The salesperson had made an honest mistake; his employment history was outstanding, and the commission was scheduled to be paid the week before Christmas. He was the salesperson mentioned earlier in the chapter—a single father with two young sons. I could not be influenced to make a decision that I believed was unjust.

These are two examples of how I often supported my staff, sometimes at the risk of my compensation. I am not suggesting that you compromise the policies and procedures set by your senior leadership team; however, a part of leadership is having the courage to make difficult decisions. Lead with kindness whenever possible. Always tell the truth. Whether it's good news or bad news, be honest. There are no secrets in your office. If you are required to keep a secret, don't disclose it to anyone. There are occasions when information is provided by senior leadership that you can't share. Remember, one of the greatest challenges of sales leadership is balancing the expectations of your staff with those of your leadership team. However, helping your team achieve results that surpass their imagination is one of its greatest rewards.

Review Questions

- Do you consider yourself a person of high integrity? If so, why?
- Who are the people in your life you consider high-integrity people, and why?
- How far would you go to support your team?
- What decision have you made as a leader that you regret the most?
- How effectively do you balance the needs of your team with those of your senior leadership?

41

Humility

Humility is when uplifting the people around you, while minimizing your importance, is your sincere motivation.

I WAS A confident leader, far from arrogant or boastful. Yet I did not completely understand the power of humility during my first few years as a sales manager. If you were to ask me, I would have said, "I'm all about the team." But success has a way of eroding your memory. The success I experienced as a sales professional afforded me a lifestyle that exceeded my expectations. My team's early success made me feel good about myself. It was a sobering experience when the market experienced a downturn, and achieving corporate goals and objectives became more challenging. The unbelievable part of the situation is that, in so many words, I asked for it. I was curious about how I would react or manage a less-than-robust sales environment.

Humility became more critical when I needed to develop a strategy to inspire my sales team to explore new products and sales customer categories. As corporate executive Suzan Nascimento said, "People don't change because they see the light, but because they feel the heat."

Some leaders fail to recognize the value of humility, regardless of the situation. They always find reasons to make the company's success their success. They struggle to realize that no one achieves any level of success without the help of others. Inflated egos have made it difficult for poor and average leaders to become good and great leaders. You didn't do it alone. Good leaders take responsibility during tough times, but credit their team during good times.

My sales teams helped create some of the most profitable radio stations in their metro survey areas. There were months when my first team's monthly revenue exceeded the yearly revenue of many of our competitors. I believed I could remain their sales manager for as long as I wished, but soon realized that was not the case. It was another valuable epiphany. I was not the station owner. Our radio station group merged with another radio group, resulting in the formation of a new company. I had to adjust to a different style of supervision. I had always led with my heart first, but never at the cost of not realizing senior leadership's expectations. I believed what was beneficial for my team most of the time was also beneficial for the company. However, my new supervisors had a different style and philosophy. They were not bad people; it was an example of a bad fit. I resisted and did a poor job of managing up, which, as highlighted in a previous chapter, is as important as managing down. The experience was profoundly humbling. I had always felt in control, and our previous company's senior leadership allowed our program director and me to make many of the station's business decisions. The new leadership team minimized our previous accomplishments and was determined to change our culture.

It wasn't the first time I had experienced a challenging situation, and I continued to believe in my ability and had the willpower to persevere. However, it became apparent that my personality and leadership style did not fit well in the new culture. I continued to work hard while looking for new employment opportunities. My current situation created a powerful epiphany: Being humble beats the heck out of being humbled.

A humble personality will help you move up the Relationship Pyramid. Exhibiting humility also makes it easier to develop friendships. Being friendly is considered a personality trait, but a friend is someone you trust and accept unconditionally. You acknowledge and understand their weaknesses as much as their strengths. Humility helps foster empathy and contributes to the development of friendships.

Humility is not synonymous with meekness. Leaders who exhibit humility are neither meek nor without pride. Being humble does not mean you should hide your accomplishments. It takes strength to be a humble leader. Be proud of your achievements, but don't wear them on your sleeve. In his book *Good to Great*, Jim Collins said, "An individual who blends extreme personal humility with intense professional will is the most effective leader."

Review Questions

- Can you share a time when your ego superseded your good common sense?
- How have you exhibited humility as a supervisor or salesperson?
- Who are some of the leaders who exhibit humility?
- When have you been humbled, and what was your reaction?
- How has your humility helped you create friendships? Give an example.

42

Finding Your Sales Sweet Spot

"Success is to be measured not so much by the position that one has reached in life as by the obstacles which he has overcome."

—Booker T. Washington

The 12 Actionable Activities

1. You are the most critical person in your life. You cannot help family, friends, or teammates if you are unwilling to invest in yourself. Enroll in self-improvement classes, emulate other successful people, read books and periodicals, and seek out mentors. Read.
2. Avoid waiting until the next day. Procrastination is a significant cause of unrealized dreams. Waiting for a better time seldom delivers the best results. A day early will always defeat a day late.
3. Be empathic. This is when you aspire to understand the other person's pain. It's your ability to feel what your customer is feeling. Put yourself in the other person's shoes. If you were the customer, how would you receive your proposed solution?
4. Work as hard on Friday as you do on Monday. Taking Friday off reduces your potential by 20 percent. Would

you agree to a 20 percent pay cut in exchange for Fridays off from work? Working Fridays is one of the best opportunities to get ahead of your competition.

5. Work to provide service that exceeds expectations. The good news is that it's often as simple as doing what you said you would do before you said you would do it. You can create an expectation. Never promise a Tuesday delivery if Thursday is acceptable.

6. Fundamentals work. Style and fundamentals are not the same. Use your style to differentiate yourself from the competition, but never forget the fundamentals. Stick to the process.

7. Success is a journey, not a destination. What made you successful today usually will not deliver future success. Use your imagination. Be an information sponge. There is a reason that no NFL team has won three consecutive Super Bowls, and only seven have won consecutive Super Bowls.

8. Remember that it all depends on you. Take responsibility for failures and credit those who helped you succeed. Yes, there will be challenging times and people. Focus on what you can control. If someone closes a door, work to open a window.

9. Finish the day smarter and better than it began. Be intentional about learning, cultivating relationships, and helping someone succeed. Help make this world a better place for everyone. Be better today than yesterday. Be intentional.

10. Use Sundays to prepare for the upcoming Monday. This is another opportunity to get ahead of your competition. Don't spend the first two hours of every Monday preparing for the week; instead, prepare on Sunday. Those two hours per week will deliver 12 additional eight-hour days over 48 weeks.

11. Remember the "power of one more." There is a lesson in understanding the power of one more. One more does not seem complicated, but it will garner results above imagination. One more sales call a day. One more attempted phone call a day. One more thank you note a day. How about getting out of bed one hour earlier per day? All can potentially increase your productivity by 20 to 30 percent.

12. Be responsible. Take full responsibility for every situation in your life. Every day, you will face obstacles. Expect and conquer. A good friend once told me, "The harder I work, the luckier I get." I never believed in luck, but he had an acronym for luck that I've shared for several years. Luck is simply: Labor Under Correct Knowledge.

Review Questions

- Do you have a competitive spirit?
- Who are the people you respect the most in your industry, and why?
- Are you willing to work as hard on Friday as you do on Monday? If not, why?
- What are a few things that you do for self-improvement?
- What are you willing to sacrifice to achieve excellence?

Conclusion:
Final Sales Sweet Spots

The book is titled *The Sales Sweet Spot*, but its use is universal. Sales is simply a value exchange, but it depends on how you interact with people. It's your ability to communicate and engage with people where they are. It doesn't matter whether you are engaging with a person on the environmental service staff or the CEO of a Fortune 100 company.

Allow fairness to be your guide. Sales is an honorable profession. As mentioned in the book's opening, many of my friends and associates are highly successful sales professionals, including my two sons. Both work in the medical sales industry. My daughter is an OB-GYN physician. The same kind of engaging people skills are necessary to succeed in her career.

I have found that when you engage with people with a kind spirit, you usually receive one in return. Take a genuine interest in all people, regardless of their beliefs or unique characteristics. According to the book of James 4:14, "Whereas you do not know what will happen tomorrow. For what is your life? It is even a vapor that appears for a little time and then vanishes away."

A sales career will enable you to meet hundreds of new and different people during your lifetime. God gave everyone an equal portion of time. Like the verse recorded in the book of James, life is short; don't waste one minute.

The following are four words starting with the letter P that are thought-producing nutrients.

- **Your Perspective** to live through: Your point of view. How do you handle problems? Do you view them as opportunities? Problems and challenges are opportunities to build character. Life is a series of hurdles. Meet them head-on. They are there to prepare you for the next hurdle.
- **Your Priority** to live by: What are your interests and desires? Discover what inspires you. Be an honest self-evaluator. Allow your passion to be your guide. Be passionate about your work and strive to achieve ambitious goals.
- **Your Purpose** to live for: What is your why? The two most significant days in your life are the day of your birth and the day you identify your purpose and why. What keeps you going? What are your values? Beliefs are powerful, but people are inspired by what they value. Does your career satisfy your purpose?
- **Your Power** to live on: I believe everyone needs a power to draw from. The blessings I have received did not come to me by accident. They are the result of hundreds of prayers. I thank God for a nurturing mother and a loving father. I am the result of their prayers. Jesus Christ has been my power for as long as I can

remember. He will answer your prayers if you give him an opportunity.

"Do not be anxious about anything, but in everything by prayer and supplication with thanksgiving let your requests be made known to God. And the peace of God, which surpasses all understanding, will guard your hearts and your minds in Christ Jesus."

—Philippians 4:6-7

Review Inquiry

Hey, it's George here.

I hope you've enjoyed the book, finding it both useful and fun. I have a favor to ask you.

Would you consider giving it a rating wherever you bought the book? Online book stores are more likely to promote a book when they feel good about its content, and reader reviews are a great barometer for a book's quality.

So please go to the website of wherever you bought the book, search for my name and the book title, and leave a review. If able, perhaps consider adding a picture of you holding the book. That increases the likelihood your review will be accepted!

Many thanks in advance,

George Demaree